# I've Been Semi-Retired Since the Day I Was Born

*Essays and Lyrics from 10 years as an unknown folksinger*

By Brad Sanzenbacher

# Blue State

I got my driver's license in the fall of 2001. At first, I was only allowed to drive between my home, school, and the homes of a few friends who lived nearby in our rural corner of Carroll County, Maryland. A few nights a week, I could also drive myself to my job at a local supermarket, where I was responsible for pushing shopping carts out of the parking lot and into the store, so they'd be available for shoppers.

Though Sisyphean in nature, pushing carts at the Super Fresh was an easy gig. I spent most of my shift wandering the tar-patched parking lot without supervision. Since Norman, the evening shift manager, was often busy nailing his doe-eyed married girlfriend in the produce room, on most nights I wasn't exactly busting my ass.

The first time I drove to work on my own, I was insufferable in drawing attention to this major life milestone. To any of my colleagues who ventured outside to smoke a cigarette, I'd parrot my unsolicited commentary on the commute. "How 'bout that traffic today?" I'd say with a chuckle. Or, "Pennsylvania drivers, am I right?" I'd let the bait hang in the air, waiting for an invitation to show off my license, while the smokers kept their eyes fixed upon the pink horizon, beyond the parked cars, and east towards the distant sea.

My final task of every shift was to clean their spent cigarettes from the ashtrays outside the store's automatic doors, and I did so dutifully just before 9pm. On my way to punch out, I'd swing by the bulk-candy aisle and fill a plastic baggie with a half-pound or so of Sour Patch Kids, and take them to my friend Jen's checkout lane, where she would ring them up as weighing only an ounce. It was an innocent scam, but Jen always played it up with a bit of theatrics. *"One little ounce of candy? Are you sure that's all you want tonight, hun?"* I'd give her my 75 cents and she'd wink at me like we were counting cards at Caesars Palace, trying our best to make sure that for once, the house didn't win.

I'd reach the time clock each night to find myself in line behind a weird assortment of characters waiting their turn to punch in. These were the late night crew: a strange, pale group of people with a wide spectrum of disfigurements. I often wondered if they had chosen to work in the stockroom at midnight, or if it was a decision made by the suits at corporate, who worried the store's family image would be harmed if it were staffed solely by hunch-backed grocers with flippers for hands. Whatever the reason, I tried to avoid eye contact and remain outside the range of their evil telepathy. Within a few moments, I'd swipe a plastic card through a machine and be on my way, leaving the stale smell of ancient linoleum floors and the infinite loop of post 9/11 patriotic soft rock behind.

Then I'd get in my car, turn the key, and the CD I was listening to on the way to work would start to play again. I'd turn the headlights on, shift into drive and pull out of the parking lot like a man who drives a car.

To this day, there's something about the way that cool night air hits my face through the open window of an accelerating car that gives

# Blue State

I got my driver's license in the fall of 2001. At first, I was only allowed to drive between my home, school, and the homes of a few friends who lived nearby in our rural corner of Carroll County, Maryland. A few nights a week, I could also drive myself to my job at a local supermarket, where I was responsible for pushing shopping carts out of the parking lot and into the store, so they'd be available for shoppers.

Though Sisyphean in nature, pushing carts at the Super Fresh was an easy gig. I spent most of my shift wandering the tar-patched parking lot without supervision. Since Norman, the evening shift manager, was often busy nailing his doe-eyed married girlfriend in the produce room, on most nights I wasn't exactly busting my ass.

The first time I drove to work on my own, I was insufferable in drawing attention to this major life milestone. To any of my colleagues who ventured outside to smoke a cigarette, I'd parrot my unsolicited commentary on the commute. "How 'bout that traffic today?" I'd say with a chuckle. Or, "Pennsylvania drivers, am I right?" I'd let the bait hang in the air, waiting for an invitation to show off my license, while the smokers kept their eyes fixed upon the pink horizon, beyond the parked cars, and east towards the distant sea.

My final task of every shift was to clean their spent cigarettes from the ashtrays outside the store's automatic doors, and I did so dutifully just before 9pm. On my way to punch out, I'd swing by the bulk-candy aisle and fill a plastic baggie with a half-pound or so of Sour Patch Kids, and take them to my friend Jen's checkout lane, where she would ring them up as weighing only an ounce. It was an innocent scam, but Jen always played it up with a bit of theatrics. *"One little ounce of candy? Are you sure that's all you want tonight, hun?"* I'd give her my 75 cents and she'd wink at me like we were counting cards at Caesars Palace, trying our best to make sure that for once, the house didn't win.

I'd reach the time clock each night to find myself in line behind a weird assortment of characters waiting their turn to punch in. These were the late night crew: a strange, pale group of people with a wide spectrum of disfigurements. I often wondered if they had chosen to work in the stockroom at midnight, or if it was a decision made by the suits at corporate, who worried the store's family image would be harmed if it were staffed solely by hunch-backed grocers with flippers for hands. Whatever the reason, I tried to avoid eye contact and remain outside the range of their evil telepathy. Within a few moments, I'd swipe a plastic card through a machine and be on my way, leaving the stale smell of ancient linoleum floors and the infinite loop of post 9/11 patriotic soft rock behind.

Then I'd get in my car, turn the key, and the CD I was listening to on the way to work would start to play again. I'd turn the headlights on, shift into drive and pull out of the parking lot like a man who drives a car.

To this day, there's something about the way that cool night air hits my face through the open window of an accelerating car that gives me goosebumps. If the backdrop happens to be the navy blue sky of a full mooned night, that's even better. These feelings were born in those days, when the car didn't mean transportation so much as liberation; from school, or work, or the awkward handshake of a girlfriend's father. Gas was a buck eighteen a gallon in 2001, and some old-timers liked to complain that was too high.

On this particular night, I needed to fill my tank with some of that sweet, cheap gasoline. My gas light was on, and while I knew how to pump gas, this would be the first time since getting my license the previous weekend that I would do it on my own. I ran through the questions in my head: *did I have cash? Yes. Which gas station would I choose? Hess is the cheapest, I think. Is that on the way home? I can drive now - everything's on the way home.*

I pulled into the Hess about a mile from the supermarket, and ever-so-cautiously inched my car to the pump. I parked and walked to the small kiosk where a clerk sat behind a glass window, and slid a ten dollar bill to him through a metal trap door. He punched a few buttons, and nodded what I thought was a signal for me to go back to the car and start pumping. With the anxiety of someone who doesn't really know what they're doing but whose only choice is to pretend, I lifted the filler off the pump, and stuck it into my gas tank. I squeezed the trigger, and -- holy smokes, it actually worked.

At the pump beside me, an old hillbilly was filling up a Dodge Ram. I was born and raised in Carroll County, and knew his type well. He wore jeans faded with dirt and muddy steel toed boots, and an unbuttoned flannel shirt over a sleeveless t-shirt; the kind of garment we used to call a "wife beater." On his head he wore a red mesh ball cap, and gnarly strands of a thinning gray mullet hung out of its sides and back. His face was hardened, more likely by liquor and maybe some meth rather than labor.

He stood with his torso perpendicular to his beater of a truck and held the nozzle tightly with both hands as he pumped the gas, so that his body and arms looked like he had been frozen mid-swing while chipping a golf ball out of a sand trap. *Who stands like that?* I thought, and I peeked one eye at him from behind my pump.

He didn't notice me. Instead, his gaze was fixed straight ahead on another car that had just pulled up to the pump ahead of his. It was a black Nissan with New Jersey plates, and from the drivers side, a young black man emerged. He was well dressed in the way a young professional might be; with dark jeans and a button down shirt underneath a slim corduroy jacket. Through the windshield, I could see a white woman sitting in the passenger seat. She was slightly younger with sandy blonde hair, and wore a white hoodie with the name of a university spelled across the front in large, collegiate type.

The black man yelled across the short gap between his car and the Dodge to get the hillbilly's attention. "Excuse me, Sir."

The old man said nothing. He just kept both hands on the gas pump, and his gaze fixed straight ahead.

"I said, excuse me sir," he repeated. "Do you know how to get to Emmitsburg from here?"

Again, the old man let the question hang in the air for a moment, then finally spoke. "I think the folks up in Emmitsburg would want you to turn around and go back where you came from."

The young man was stunned, and for a moment, said nothing. "What did you say to me?" he said when he finally spoke.

"I said, I think you should turn around and go back where you came from," the hillbilly repeated without affect, as though he were simply giving the man the time.

The young man turned around to face the white woman, and shrugged his arms in frustration. She opened the passenger side door of the car, and stood up behind it, leaning on the window for support.

"What did he say?" she whispered, sensing her friend was upset. I could hear the hint of a New Jersey accent in her voice.

"I think you're running with the wrong crowd," the hillbilly yelled to her, unprompted.

"I'm sorry, what the fuck did you just say to me?" she said, loudly this time, and her accent became more pronounced.

"I said -" the old man began, and she cut him off.

"No. No. What the fuck did you just say to me?" She repeated, and stepped out from behind the car door with several swift steps towards the Dodge.

"Kelly, don't!" the young man yelled after her, and tried to hold her back as she marched forward. "Let's just go."

"I said you're running with the wrong crowd," the hillbilly snarled, and almost immediately, the girl was in his face, screaming. He didn't flinch.

What she said exactly, I don't remember. She had tears in her eyes as she yelled, and behind her, her friend did as well. His elbows were high in the air as he gripped the top of his head with his hands, and tried to remain calm while still trying to coax her back towards the car. But she didn't budge, and finally the old man sneered again.

"You better control your girl," he said, and confidently moved his left hand from the handle of his gas pump to his hip, where he rested it on something concealed beneath the flannel shirt that hung loosely from his torso.

The yelling halted immediately, and the girl and the young man froze as though time itself had stopped. The silence was finally broken by the deafening click of my gas pump shutting off when my $10 were spent and gone.

"Kelly. Let's go," the young man repeated with desperation in his voice

"Please. Just get in the car."

She obeyed, and in a few seconds, the Nissan was rolling backwards, and I was staring hard through its windshield, trying to lock eyes with either of its occupants, hoping to convey a silent apology through the glass. *I'm sorry*, I wanted to say. *We're not all like this. Please.* But their gazes stayed fixed on the old man's boney hand that hovered above his waistline.

When their car had cleared the curb and sped off, I peered from behind the pump and looked over at the man. He calmly pulled the fuel nozzle out of his tank and replaced it on the pump, then whistled a tune as he walked to the kiosk to collect his change. It was only then that I noticed the boy who sat on the passenger side of the truck's bench seat, no more than 8 years old, who watched with wide, worried eyes through the dirty windshield.

I got in my own car and started it, and pulled again onto the potholed highway. The night air hit my face through the open window and it felt like a liberation, and as I drove beneath the navy sky, I ate candy with fingers that smelled like gasoline. I thought about the couple in the Nissan, and wondered if I would be the story when they retold it. More importantly, I wondered whose side I'd be on.

## *Love Minus Zero*

I hold my grudges very dear to my heart. I nourish them and give them attention, and like pets, I dread their loss and grieve when they inevitably fade away. Before long, I'll bring home a new one, and my wife will try in vain to convince me I can't keep it.

I care so deeply for my grudges because I'm selective when it comes to forming them. Not all unpleasant interactions are worthy of 20 years of my unrelenting spite, so I let a lot of things go. Human error or incompetence, I'm pretty forgiving about. I've messed up plenty of jobs in my life, so I can't get too upset when a hotel loses my reservation or a restaurant sends me the wrong meal.

People who accidentally cause me harm also can be forgiven, as can people who harm me deliberately. The specifics of the episode matter, of course, but my general rule is: if we're going to look back on something and laugh about it someday, we might as well start now.

The people who get to me the most, the grudgeworthy ones, are the clueless ones. The people who swerve through life without checking their mirrors, oblivious to the wreckage they leave in their wake. For them, I reserve a very particular and aggressive form of loathing.

Standing on the left side of the escalator at the subway station? *God help me, I'll throw you in front of a train.*

Texting at a green arrow so I have to sit through the light again? *I'll nail the doors to your house shut and burn it to the ground.*

Of course, I've never actually cast someone into the path of a subway train or committed any fatal acts of arson, but when a stranger so blithely ignores the clearest rules of polite society, my thoughts tend to gather in a pattern typical of a psychopath or a violent criminal. This might be because of my deep love for my fellow man: I can't stand it when people are discourteous and inattentive to the needs of others. It's also possible that spite is more of a hobby to me than a genuine affliction, and that I actively seek out reasons to practice it.

One of my biggest grudges in life is reserved for my elementary school music teacher, Mrs. Isaacs, who succeeded in teaching me that music is nothing more than a joyless expression of state-mandated curriculum. In her class, we learned to play the recorder, a flute-like instrument that's widely known for its role in grade school music, but otherwise is just a piece of plastic that could have been a soda bottle or a dildo; anything would be more usefully, really.

I couldn't figure out the recorder for a number of reasons. In elementary school, I generally struggled with reading, so trying to make sense of music on paper was difficult. And when it came to fingering the notes, my less than stellar fine motor skills didn't give me a lot of precision.

These handicaps were concealable during our group lessons, where I was able to hold the recorder in my mouth and pantomime playing along. I did so hoping we'd stick with the recorder unit for a few weeks, then move on to something else, never to revisit it again.

What I didn't know was that there would be a test at the end that was uniquely impervious to my skill of acing tests without really knowing the material.

For the recorder test, each student had to stand by Mrs. Isaacs' piano and perform a song directly to her, reading music from a sheet. On test day, my brow beaded with sweat as I watched my classmates file to the front of the room one by one and conjure melodic little toots from their recorders with varying degrees of skill. Mostly, they were competent enough to earn mild praise from Mrs. Isaacs as she sent them back to their seats.

When it was my turn, I made a slow march across the killing floor and planted my feet beside the upright piano. With 25 pairs of eyes and ears focused only on me, I silently prayed we'd be interrupted by gunfire in the hallway.

Mrs. Isaacs turned the page of her music book to a song titled "Indian March," and I scanned the meaningless music notation briefly as I drew the recorder to my mouth. When I blew into the instrument, what came out was unrecognizable as music, and only barely within the envelope of sound tolerable to the human ear. If I played a single note correctly, it was purely by accident.

Mrs. Isaacs sat unflinching through my recitation, as if insisting without words that I stand there, finish the song and soak in my shame the way god intended. When I was done, she stared at me with a deep, ambivalent cruelty. "I'm going to have to give you an F," she said, then motioned me back to my chair, where I took my seat, thinking only about how badly I never wanted to hear or attempt to create music ever again.

From that day forward, music made me insecure and I tried to avoid it. If my friends were talking about their favorite bands, I'd make an excuse to leave. *There are too many bands, anyway,* I'd tell myself. *How is anyone supposed to keep track of them all?*

This remained true until I was 13 or so. In middle school, my friends had a band called the Sock Monkeys, and they played a few gigs a year at family gatherings. I loved being around their band, and the classic rock covers they played introduced me to a lot of music that I still listen to today. One song in their repertoire was "Rebel Rebel" by David Bowie, and I liked their version so much that I bought Bowie's album "The Rise and Fall of Ziggy Stardust and the Spiders from Mars" shortly after hearing it. It wasn't the record with "Rebel Rebel" on it, but the cover art drew me in.

The opening track of that record is called "Five Years," and it immediately opened a door in my mind. It's got a crunchy drum kit and an orchestral piano, and the bass sounds like it comes from deep in space. More importantly, I was obsessed with the way the lyrics and the melody brought a scene to life like watching a movie. I've listened to that album hundreds of times, and I still see "Five Years" in my mind they way I did the first time I heard it.

Even as I was falling deeper and deeper in love with music, undoing the oblivious tragedy inflicted by Mrs. Isaacs, I still didn't have any faith in my ability to make it myself. I was in a band briefly in high school as the singer (we formed just to play the school talent show then never played again), and I tried taking guitar lessons once, but that didn't last long. Every time I tried to make music, I struggled. And every time, I'd think back to the recorder test, and remember that I had no natural talent. Mrs. Isaacs had confirmed this as a fact.

In 2006, I registered for a class at college called "Bob Dylan: Iconic

Iconoclast." I registered because I had been a casual fan of Dylan for many years, and thought it may be an easy class to fill out my senior year. I also knew my friend John Nagle would be in it, and he and I could bullshit about anything, all day long.

It turned out that the class wasn't so easy. Our professor, James Salvucci, was a lifelong Dylan fan and he challenged us with difficult writing assignments to interpret Dylan's songs. We listened to his entire catalogue, and as a result, I was exposed to a lot of music I'd never heard, or at least, had never listened to closely. One such song was "Love Minus Zero (No Limit)" from the 1965 album "Bringing It All Back Home."

"Love Minus Zero" is a great song, but not one of Dylan's bigger hits. It's an important early example of the surrealist Dylan we'd see cranking out records for the next few years. Like "Five Years," it painted a picture in my head so clearly that I felt like I was walking through the streets of New York City in the '60s.

The simplicity of "Love Minus Zero" is what made it stand out to me. I wasn't intimidated by it. It was both beautiful and accessible. I didn't know what notes or chords Dylan was strumming on his guitar, but I could tell there weren't very many of them. Structurally, there was no chorus or bridge. The phrase "Love Minus Zero" wasn't even in the song. Just a few scenes over a few verses, written by someone who walked through the world and paid attention to the same kinds of things that I felt I paid attention to.

As I listened to "Love Minus Zero" over and over, a strange thought crept into my mind. It was a thought that hadn't once occurred to me since the recorder test or through many years of listening closely to the bands that had become a big part of my life. When I heard that song, I thought, *I could probably do that.*

Bob Dylan is considered to be one of the most important English language writers since Shakespeare. He has won every award imaginable, sold millions of records, and had his songs covered thousands of times by everyone from Jimi Hendrix to Adele. He began playing music as a teenager, and by the time he was 22 years old (my age at the time) he was already well into his deal with Columbia records. For me to think, *I could probably do that* with no musical talent and years behind schedule, was utterly insane.

I had a Takamine Jasmine guitar in my closet from when I'd taken lessons in high school, and one day I dusted it off. I bought a book called "How to Play Guitar in Every Key" and used it to learn chord progressions, then started to understand how songs could be transposed from one key to another.

I'd practice at every possible minute, methodically, moving my fingers from G to C over and over for hours. Then from C to D for hours. The Jasmine had terrible action and was difficult to play, but I practiced until my fingertips were calloused and the tendons in my wrist seethed with pain.

The late comedian Mitch Hedberg had a joke that goes, "I taught myself how to play guitar, which was a bad decision because I didn't know how to play it. So I was a shitty teacher."

Like Mitch, I was a shitty teacher and am still a pretty bad guitar player. What I lacked in knowledge I made up for with brute force, and worked tirelessly until I'd see small improvements. To this day, I can't solo, can barely play scales in some keys, and I know next to nothing about music theory.

I sometimes regret that I'm not a better musician but I also know that the standards of being a great player were out of reach for me. Had I held myself to that standard of excellence, I would have quit playing after a few tries. The mountain was too tall. Like the recorder, I would have felt the struggle and never seen the progress, and chosen silence over practice.

Besides: my target wasn't *ElectricLadyLand* or *Clapton Unplugged*. It was "Love Minus Zero," a simple folk song with strummed guitar and a wild orange sky of surrealist lyrics.

I had been playing guitar for about three months when I composed my first song, called "Soldier of Fortune." It felt good to play it over and over and burn it into my memory, and I loved the ease of writing it. I had just finished a degree in film and video production, and was feeling burned out by how much work it is to tell a story through film. You needed a polished script, a crew, actors, lights, sound: it costs a fortune and takes years. After a few months of practicing, however, I could tell a story through songwriting, and all I needed was a guitar and my voice.

Of course, singing was another new skill that I had to teach myself, and it made me feel more vulnerable than playing guitar. My singing was terrible at the start and would remain that way for many years. At least by performing consistently, I was able to feel more confident and learn to sing in a way that, if not correct, was at least bearable.

The first time I played an open mic was in Gettysburg, Pennsylvania. I chose Gettysburg because it was far enough away that I could be almost certain no one I knew would be there. More so than my skill level, I was embarrassed by the fact that I wanted to be on-stage; or thought that was something I could do.

When I left my parents' house, I tiptoed my guitar out the front door and slipped it into the trunk of my car like I was hiding a body. It was August, and I drove north through the corn fields and across the Mason Dixon line, all while devising a cover story in case I saw someone I knew.

Fortunately, the open mic was new and the only people in the audience were the 19-year-old host and his mother. It was a good crowd in my opinion, and since there was no long list of performers, they let me play all three of the songs I knew, twice.

After the open mic I drove home through the cool night air that hovered above the blue and white fields. I knew that I hadn't been good, but I didn't feel embarrassed about it. I had told the host and his mother it was my first time playing, and they told me they liked my songs and my lyrics and that they hoped I would stick with it. In the car, I thought about Mrs. Isaacs and wondered where I would be if her reaction to my failed recorder test had been similar.

At the time, I had no idea that this obsession would hit me as hard as it did. But for the first time in my life playing music, I felt like I could be better. In fact, I could see it every day. The improvement was steady but still tantalizing; every ounce of progress made me want more. It felt good to be sticking with it, and better to see results.

I listened to nothing but Dylan that whole summer, and his words echoed in my mind. Dylan's music, in my mind, is the music of resilience. From "Tangled Up in Blue," to "Hurricane," to "Blowing in the wind," there is a consistent theme that life can be hard, but we are capable of surviving our hardships. I thought about that as I'd lament my regret and eventually let my anger towards Mrs. Isaacs fade away. I had the choice to keep pressing forwards now, and no amount of shame from my past could stop me.

"He not being born is busy dying," Dylan says. And for the first time in my life, I felt like I was busy being born.

# Fear and Drought

Shortly after graduating college with a degree in film, I told my parents I was thinking about becoming a folk singer. This was a crazy thing for me to say. I had never played an instrument or sung in my life, and on the few occasions I had tried, didn't demonstrate an aptitude for either. Had I told my parents I was thinking about becoming a time-traveling assassin, they may have worried about my ability to earn a steady living. The idea I could become a folk singer, however, was too absurd to dignify with genuine objections.

That's because for the majority of my life, my main hobby had been quitting things. I joined the Cub Scouts at age eight and quit when I realized I didn't particularly care how the flag was folded. I quit karate after one lesson because the instructor kept going on and on about respect and discipline. I quit the Civil Air Patrol and religion for basically those same reasons.

I've come to see that there were two main reasons I'd quit things. The first was that they required being in the same place at the same time every week. *Lessons? Teams? Clubs?* These things were begging to be quit on the basis of commitment alone.

The other reason I'd quit a thing was if I didn't appear to be immediately good at it, and didn't enjoy it enough to practice and improve.

When I was 10, my favorite activity was riding my bike in circles and imagining horrific ways the kids who bullied me at school might die. Each day I'd craft an elaborate new fantasy about molten lava or falling boulders, and I cackled to myself as I imagined the little fucker's mullet-headed parents watching as their rat-tailed child was crushed, impaled, or otherwise decapitated. Looking back, it wasn't a healthy thing to do, and it certainly wasn't something my parents would have endorsed. Fortunately no lessons were needed: I was just fine on my own.

That's why the thought that at age 22, I would find the discipline to learn to play guitar, and then learn to sing, and then learn to write songs, and then somehow combine these skills, was completely ridiculous.

For a while, it really seemed that way. I was living at home at the time, and my parents could hear me practice every day. Our golden retriever would make a beeline for the door when I picked up my guitar, and my visiting grandmother asked me if I had ever thought about voice lessons. These were both appropriate responses to the prison-torture sound my vocal chords produced when I'd sing; trying to match the yipping styles of folk singers like Woody Guthrie, Ramblin' Jack Elliott, or a young Bob Dylan.

I spent the Summer after graduation working nights as a video crew member for the Baltimore Orioles, which was a low paying but enjoyable part-time job that I had been working for a few baseball seasons. I was also a camp counselor for a few weeks, and worked a variety of sporadic video gigs for people I had known through the

Orioles. When I didn't have any work, I'd spend the days browsing the internet for jobs with benefits, and trying to find as much time as possible to practice guitar and build strength in my voice.

As the summer began to fade, the Orioles' season reliably faded with it. October would bring the end of my only stable employment, and my anxiety about earning money was overshadowed by the joy of having more time to practice music.

But I knew myself well enough to know I'd likely fall victim to my own "yes" cycle, and end up filling my time with garbage video gigs, driving hours across Maryland to work for people who, if I was lucky, might get around to paying me sometime in the next 6 months. I decided to free myself by spending the month of October at my parent's vacation property in Canaan Valley, West Virginia.

The plan was to put distance between myself and my tendency towards selling my time for twelve dollars an hour. I also wanted to go someplace where there were fewer distractions - just for a little while - to focus on practicing guitar and singing. I had friends who spent years after college backpacking through Europe or Asia, so one month without working or looking for work didn't seem unreasonable. The day after baseball season ended, I hit the road.

There's a point in western Maryland, near a town called Hancock, at which the state is barely a mile wide from north to south. At the southern border is the Potomac river, and beyond that a vast expanse of West Virginia's mountain country. The northern border is the Mason-Dixon line, which separates Maryland from Pennsylvania. It's in this narrow point of Maryland that I-68 splits from I-70, and heads due west towards Cumberland and into the heart of Appalachia. The 10 mile stretch of I-68 following that split will forever, in my mind, be linked to Son Volt's "Windfall."

> *May the wind take your troubles away*
> *May the wind take your troubles away*
> *Both feet on the floor, two hands on the wheel,*
> *May the wind take your troubles away*
> *Trying to make it far enough, to the next time zone*
> *Few and far between past the midnight hour*
> *Never feel alone, you're really not alone*

In fact, I would stab the album into my car's CD player just before exiting I-70, so that it synced perfectly with the road approaching Sideling Hill, which is a 100 meter notch cut into the Allegheny mountains by the industrious little scamps of a bygone era. I can see them in their coveralls and little helmets - toting their lunch pails around as they dynamited and hydraulicked their way through the ancient appalachian sediment to make way for the snaking freeway; and boy, what a job they had done.

It's far enough outside out of reasonable commute range from the Baltimore and DC suburbs, in a part of the country where nearly every pickup truck on the road was fitted with a strange rack for hauling off the carcasses of animals shot by the driver. After now living for years in California it's laughable to say: but to me, this was the wild west.

I was heading to Thomas and Davis in West Virginia, which are two old coal towns that share a main street, about 2 miles from each other in the state's eastern panhandle. They are isolated communities in the Appalachian sense; about an hour from the nearest Wal-Mart or full-sized grocery store. This doesn't sound that bad until you imagine planning your week around which days you'll be "going into town", and carefully making lists of items that you need to bring back. It's not primitive by any stretch, but it does make you realize there are conveniences you take for granted in suburbs and cities.

Nearby is Canaan Valley, which is just that: an expanse between two mountains with two ski resorts and a few thousand acres of protected forest and grassland in the Blackwater Rivershed. It's in this valley that my parents owned a house that we used for a few weeks a year as a vacation property.

My only real plan here was to sit alone and practice, and to work on singing without fear of making anyone cringe. But I also knew that Thomas was a regional music hub. The Purple Fiddle brought touring bluegrass acts five nights a week, and a few other breweries had local music regularly. So the hope, I suppose, was that I would find these people.

I found them at the Mountain State Brewery, which hosted an open jam on Thursday nights. Today, there are few words more frightening to me than "open jam." Fortunately, back then I was naive about how bad I was at playing the guitar.

That naiveté was resolved quickly, thanks to some old pickers who could really play. I tried to follow along anyway, and over the weeks began to pick up common chord progressions and structures that made up Appalachian songs. I got the point where I could change chords faster and faster, and eventually could even anticipate the changes of songs as I was playing them for the first time. The brewery smelled like cold beer and campfire, and I played guitar wearing gloves with their fingers cut off.

That month I was exposed to traditional songs I had never heard before in my cable-age suburban home. "The New River Train" was a local favorite, and so were "Rocky Top", "Mountain Dew", and "Rolling in my Sweet Baby's Arms". They also played a haunting version of Gershwin's "Summertime", and Gillian Welch's "Look at Miss Ohio". It's here that I first heard "Wagon Wheel", which in 2007, hadn't yet been covered by Darius Rucker or overtaken Oasis's "Wonderwall" as the most popular (and hated) open mic song of all time.

The jam was made up of a regular cast of characters who would come in every week. There was Jared, the banjo player, who shaved his beard halfway through the month, and I spent the next 2 weeks thinking was someone else. ("Where's Jared been?" I asked him.) There was a mandolin, an upright bass, and a fiddle player, as well as three or four different guitar players. But "they," first and foremost, was Ben Nelson, the farmer that locals called a legend, who was the group's lead singer. Until Ben arrived, the jam was just a group of guys drinking beer and tuning up. When he got there, it became a party.

When Ben sang, his whole body rocked. From the waist up, he'd lean back and forth in time with the song, as if playing an invisible timpani with his forehead. It was slower than a head bang, and more like his body was bobbing in a very rough sea. His voice was unusual: he wasn't a yipper like I had been trying to be. He sang in more of a holler, and by mimicking his style I was able to shake some of my bad habits while adopting others.

The most important thing about Ben to me was that he was very kind. At most open jams with serious players, it's a major faux-pas to show up and suck as badly as I did. This group was only as serious as Ben let them be, and he called out chord changes for me when I was lagging behind (which I always was) and also showed me the strumming patterns if I struggled to pick them up (which I always did). He taught me how to mute my strings with my hand after a strum to get a 'boom chicka boom chicka" sound. Thanks to Ben's micro lessons, going to the open jam every week became an easy way to measure my improvements.

When I wasn't at the open jam, I was at the house practicing. I was fortunate that it rained at least 20 days that month and the cable was out. I couldn't distract myself if I wanted to.

I felt a sense of urgency to improve at the guitar and write songs as quickly as I could. In my mind, I had started late in life, and I had to make up for lost time by cramming all the practice I would have gotten if I had started at say, age 13, into a few weeks. In hindsight, it was a bad idea and it didn't work. But in the short term I was seeing gains: more chords. Faster strumming. Alternating bass notes. Boom, Chicka, Boom, Chicka, Boom, Chicka. *What else is there?*

My comfort with the guitar was coming along, but the writing was not. When you only know a few chords and you've exclusively listened to Bob Dylan for almost a year, you don't have a lot of range as a composer. I wrote one song the second week I was there called "In the Milky Way Tonight," and I wrote it specifically to force myself to practice the F-Chord. "Milky Way" is an early example of the down-on-my-luck folk lullaby that I'd come to write often in the years since. The verses, as they were written at the time are:

> *I'm far away from where I want to be*
> *And I should really be in bed*
> *Where I need to be is on a stage somewhere*
> *But by all accounts, I should be dead*
> *I've survived things against all reason*

*And I've never once taken advice*
*I'm tired today*
*And I wish I could lay*
*in the Milky Way tonight*

*I've never been so lost before*
*without trying to get found*
*but if I can stay lost just for a while more*
*Then I might just find my sound*
*My voice is a little bit scratchy*
*And my fingertips are white*
*But I'll practice today*
*and I might get to play*
*in milky way tonight*

*I watch as water slowly drips*
*From the faucet to the sink*
*My hands are stained and my page is smudged*
*With a whole pen's worth of ink*
*But these words don't seem worth keeping*
*and my brains not working right*
*Now I'm drifting away*
*and I'm burning my pay*
*in the milky way tonight*

It's a bit dramatic, but it does describe what I was feeling: exhausted frustration with a dose of hope. At the time I was proud of its simplicity and honesty, and how it relied on images to drive the mood, rather than descriptions of feelings. I felt I'd tapped into something that I'd been missing for a long time, and now that I'd done it once, I wanted more.

In my final week in West Virginia, In the "Milky Way Tonight" was still the only song I'd written. Two weeks had passed with nothing new. This had to change.

Maybe it's because I was spending most of my time alone or because I had been retraining my muscles for 18 hours a day for weeks, but I was starting to lose grip of reality. While practicing at 3 am one morning, I had what I felt was a once in a lifetime, stroke of genius idea. *If I could watch the sunrise over the ocean,* I thought, *the beauty would inspire me to write a great song.* It was that simple: my lack of results were not for lack of skill or experience - just a lack of inspiration.

The challenge of course, was geography. In Maryland, I almost certainly could have reached the ocean, or at least the shore of the Chesapeake Bay by dawn. In West Virginia, that wasn't the case. But I did know that the Appalachians were full of river valleys that had been dammed and flooded during the great depression, and I figured there had to be a pretty big lake out there, somewhere.

This was before Google Maps and long before I had anything other than a flip phone for communication. All I had was a phone book, and on the first page inside of that was a crude, hand drawn map of West Virginia. Sure enough, not too far away, a potato-shaped outline near a place called Grafton was clearly labeled Tygart Lake. I had never heard of Tygart Lake or been to Grafton, but I traced the roads with my finger, and figured I could be there in about 2 hours.

It was 3:10 A.M. when I got in my car and started driving south on the mountain roads towards Elkins. It was a kind of crisp black dark outside that most people rarely experience, and the milky way stretched across the sky like a giant dome.

Had I possessed a better map, I would have known I was not taking the shortest route. If I'd had a bigger map, it would have reminded me that Deep Creek Lake in Maryland was far closer to Canaan Valley than Tygart Lake. There's also a chance that I knew both of those things and chose to take the path of most adventure. I honestly don't remember.

You drive through a lot of unoccupied land in West Virginia. There are places like Dolly Sods Wilderness that have the words "Wilderness" right there in the title. Then there are other places like Bickle Knob, where you have to know the wilderness when you see it. There are towns that aren't really towns; bookended by signs that say you're entering and exiting, but what exactly, you're not sure. There are areas with remoteness and poverty that many people don't know exists in this country. And then there are half rejuvenated towns where, in the daylight hours, bearded young people play cornhole outside small breweries. There are historical markers telling you that Stonewall Jackson's army camped here or Anna Jarvis went to school here. There are gas stations with their pumps shut off for the night. There are even signs cautioning you to look out for Bigfoot, or encouraging you attend the tent revival that coming Sunday. I saw them all on the drive to Grafton.

Near Elkins, a Coke machine stood alone on a concrete slab by the road and glowed in the night. In need of caffeine, I stopped to buy a can. When the machine ate my last dollar, I drove away fueled instead by an orange rage; the kind of fire I used to feel on my bike, thinking about those bullies back in school.

At 6 am, I checked the math and confirmed my suspicion that the drive had in fact been longer than 2 hours. The map I'd ripped from the phone book sat on my lap, and I could tell I was heading in the right direction. *Just a little bit further,* I thought. *Endless inspiration, coming right up.* Mental exhaustion was setting in. I realized this when I sat at the flashing red light of a railroad crossing for 2 whole minutes, waiting for it to turn green.

At 6:20 am, I saw a sign pointing me towards Lake Tygart State Park, and I rolled past the empty fee booth at the entrance a few minutes later. I was surprised by how dark the sky still was. 6:20 was hardly the middle of the night, but we were far west in the time zone, and there were no hints of dawn on the horizon; only blackness and stars.

There was also no lake visible through the forest, so I followed signs pointing me towards campgrounds, thinking there was sure to be lake access there. I drove through one campground but didn't see any water or symbols for water (a sign for a boat ramp, for example). I stayed on the road as it bowed slowly to the right, but saw nothing but forest. After a mile, it was starting to feel ridiculous. With frustration amplified by exhaustion, I decided to park beside a small game trail that cut through the forest edge. I exited the car and began to walk the trail. There was still no hint of dawn.

After one hundred yards or so, the forest opened up into a large field that sloped downhill as I walked. *Any minute now,* I thought, expecting the lake to open up after the next crest. At some point, I noticed the field I was walking in didn't have any grass. I could kick the ground with the toe of my boot, and feel the hardness of the dirt. I glance behind me, and could tell the forest edge I had exited was now far away. In front of me in the distance, I could see three red lights blinking high above my head, connected by the dark outline of a mass that obscured the stars in the black sky.

*Shit.*

I realized then that the field was the lake. It had been drained for some stupid reason, and I stood upon its bed like an idiot prospector, searching for inspiration in the dry ground of its rocky bottom. In front of me stood the tall concrete structure of Tygart Dam, with its red safety lights blinking in the quiet autumn morning. I suddenly became aware that it was very cold.

My plan of watching the glory of the sunrise on a sparkling body of water had failed spectacularly, and with it, my search for inspiration in the beauty of the new day. I sat on a rock in the lake bed and rested my elbows on my knees and my chin in my palms, and stared out towards the treeline beneath the morning stars for a very long time.

And if my memory is correct (and it usually is), the sun never rose that day, either.

# A Grainy Silhouette

When I accepted a job offer at Howard County Government Television in February of 2008, I knew it was a dead end. The station had just been defunded by the county's Board of Commissioners, and as such, its small staff had found other jobs and moved on. I didn't have any better options, so I accepted the apocalyptic task of operating the channel alone for the next three months until its final broadcast date. It wasn't exactly the job I was hoping for, but they offered it to me on the spot after a short interview, and I drove home happy to have it.

I'd been searching for a job for several months and in most cases, my interviews followed a similar storyline: I would be passed over because I was young, but my interviewer would like me enough to introduce me to someone else who had an opening. In this way, I was perpetually being reminded that I was a likable but ultimately unhirable piece of garbage. In Howard County government, I'd found the perfect opportunity to prove them wrong. I could challenge myself, take ownership of a project, and still have failure guaranteed. It was poetic, really.

I reported to my first day of work the following Monday, and was told to drive to the county administration building down the street to complete some paperwork. There, I sat on a government chair from the era of the space race with a clipboard on my knee, writing my name and social security number over and over, and checking boxes about my medical and criminal history. "Do you have a known history of mental illness?" *I think I'm sane enough to run a government television station into the ground, but thanks for asking.*

When I was near the end of the paperwork my cell phone rang, and a woman on the line offered me a very similar job at an educational television station in neighboring Baltimore County, where I had also recently interviewed. This job had the major benefit of not coming to a predetermined conclusion in a few months, and so accepting it was a no brainer. I stood from the linoleum chair and informed the woman at Howard County's HR desk that I wouldn't be proceeding. She said "okay" with an ambivalence that made me wonder if this was fairly common.

A few weeks later, I started with Baltimore County. The Education Channel was a cable television station operated by the school system, and it served as a PR engine for the administration that ran the district. The dozen times a year the superintendent visited a school, the Education Channel would be there with cameras rolling to capture the scene as he knelt beside a student's desk and made polite conversation. The station also produced a sports show that highlighted the district's top athletes, a news show about projects students were working on, and a live show called Math Homework Helpers, on which a mixed cast of puppets and children offered homework help to kids at home who would call in. It was an appealing place in that it combined two of my favorite things: being creative, and driving around in an unmarked van.

My first week at the Education Channel, a colleague named John came to my desk and engaged in chit-chat for a few minutes. We talked about the usual stuff: Where'd I go to college? Where was I from? Where else had I worked? John was in his early 50s and had been with the channel for 20 years. He had begun with the county as a landscaper, and used that job to pay his way through school and move into television production. He was a huge fan of Bruce Springsteen, and we talked about music for a minute.

When he had picked over my brain to his satisfaction, he wrapped up the conversation. "Well, welcome," he said. "You'll find everyone here has each other's back." Then he leaned backwards out of my cubicle to check that the coast was clear, then leaned in close to my face to add, with a whisper, "...in their crosshairs." I laughed, assuming he was joking.

The Education Channel was built into the back of a cold-war era high school in a city called Towson. I'd arrive to work each morning, park in the back of the brown brick building, and enter through an unmarked door at the top of a concrete stoop. Inside the door was the desk of a very sweet admin named Jenny, where an ancient black and white television sat on a metal filing cabinet in the corner. A video feed from a security camera on the stoop was displayed on the television, and since there were no others at the station, they called this "the window." Staring into the window was a popular pastime at the Educational Channel.

A windowless office has a tendency to attract some characters, and though there were only about eight people on staff at the channel, it didn't disappoint. The channel was programmed each day by a very obese man who worked in a closet and had an impressive ability to bounce back from a heart attack after missing just a day or two of work. His bowel movements remain the most inhuman thing I've ever smelled, and I committed his bathroom schedule to memory so as to avoid the area during or immediately after his morning shit.

Another gentleman had actual Tourette Syndrome, which I correctly diagnosed after the fifth or sixth time I heard him aggressively scream the word "beaver" at a teenage girl. Aside from this condition, he was a nice guy, and he taught me to tie some common knots he used around the studio. He knew a lot about knots because he was also a volunteer firefighter. I liked to imagine him rushing into burning buildings and screaming "BEAVER" as he carried women out over his shoulder.

There were a few other people on staff at the education channel, most of whom were generally nice, including Todd Porter, who years later would tragically die of cancer very young. He and I would play catch together at lunch, and he was always very supportive.

Though individually everyone was nice enough, as a team, there were cracks. People guarded their work, and I was encouraged to mind my own business and not ask a lot of questions. Pitching new ideas wasn't really allowed, and if people got the impression you were trying to shake things up, you'd hear about it. The staff didn't trust each other, nor did they want to see each other outside of work, or even eat lunch together.

For a number of reasons, it became clear early on that I wasn't excelling there. There were a lot of factors to blame, which we might sum up by saying that consciously or not, I was mostly unable to hide my misery.

I dropped some video gear twice in one day in front of John, who

I could tell was documenting the incidents in his mind. I went on shoots several times and came back with footage the producers said was garbage. I took the side mirror off a Mercedes with the station's van. These were honest mistakes and not punkish, but I couldn't seem to break the cycle. I knew things were bad when I walked by an editing suite one day to see a producer reviewing footage I'd shot, and hanging his head in disappointment. I've since come to see that there were things they could have done to better coach me for success, and that culturally, the place was hostile. But when I was 23 years old, knowing that they disliked me affected me deeply.

This was amplified one day when I brought my guitar to work with me so that I could play at an open mic afterwards in Baltimore. It was a brutally hot Maryland summer day, and I carried the guitar into the office to store in my cubicle so it wouldn't bake in my car.

John saw the guitar and at lunch, insisted through a smug grin that I play a song. I had only been playing guitar for about a year, and I knew I wasn't that good. But he was joined by another coworker in his insistence, and I agreed to play for them. The rest of the office was gathered around the window, and John called them over while I tuned up.

I played a song called "You're My Best Friend by Default," which I had recently finished writing. It's a sad folk waltz about rejection, and I don't think I played it to make a statement; it was just my newest song, which in my mind made it my best.

My coworkers all listened politely, and for the most part, gave me some half-hearted applause before wandering away and back to their business. John stood back until the others had left, and smirked for a moment with self-satisfaction. "I wouldn't quit your day job," he told me.

I folded my arms on the top of my guitar. "Well John," I said, and paused for a moment to sigh. "This is my day job, and it's not really going that great either."

Around this time, I saw a musician named Billy Harvey play a show at a small cafe in the city called the Baltimore Chop. Billy was a touring songwriter from Austin, and in between songs he spoke about that city like it were El Dorado. "Austin is full of songwriters," he said. "We all get together once a week and workshop together. It's a great community." Listening to Billy gush about his songwriter friends underscored something that I was beginning to realize: I didn't really know a lot of other musicians.

I was living in my parents house in a town all my friends had left, and the Education Channel was effectively crushing my spirit. If there were other folk singers in the Baltimore area, I didn't have a lot of energy to find them. Mostly, I went to the few hip-hop heavy open mics in the city, or spent evenings at home alone, writing in the basement.

But Austin, man; that place had it all. I bet a guy could carry his guitar from bar to bar there, and play 2 or 3 open mics on a single night. And if you did well enough, they'd book you to play a full set on Friday. And on lazy sundays, you'd sit on a dusty sofa in someone's sunlit living room, drinking whiskey and swapping songs until the sun went down. These were the fantasies that ran through my head each day at the Education Channel, as I continued to make mistakes and inch myself closer to the cliff.

One day, myself and two other staff members, Craig and Patricia, had to visit a power plant on the far side of the county for a shoot. It was for a segment on a show meant to teach kids about career paths available in the area, and this piece was about the energy industry. Patricia was the producer, and Baltimore Gas & Electric had agreed to let us shoot at their facility and interview a few members of their staff for a couple hours.

When we arrived at the power plant, I was surprised to be greeted by a man named Kevin Thornton, who I'd met several times because his wife Susan was a coworker of mine from a previous job, and someone I considered a good friend. Kevin worked in communications for the utility, and was the contact with whom Pat had coordinated our shoot.

Kevin gave us a short tour of the facility, and showed us a room he had reserved for us to shoot interviews in. It was a large, industrial room with some visually interesting equipment, and he had the HVAC system turned off for several hours so we could record sound in relative quiet. He made a frame with his hands and held it in front of his face, and suggested a few places we might set the camera to make the facility look like an exciting place to work.

I thought the room looked great, so I set my gear down and started to drop the legs of my tripod. Craig and Pat looked unsatisfied. They each voiced similar complaints about how the room didn't look industrial enough, and asked if there was any place that looked more like a power plant.

"Well - this is a power plant," Kevin explained, calmly. "This is what power plants look like."

The two of them sucked air into their cheeks, and made the scrunched up, apologetic "please" faces that people tend to make when they realize they need an even bigger favor than the one they're already getting.

Kevin nodded politely, and walked us down a corridor to another room, which in my opinion, was similar. There was a loud rumble of industrial HVAC, and Kevin made a phone call that resulted in the system being shut off. He and I watched Craig and Patricia's faces, and again, their dissatisfaction was apparent.

Before either of them could speak, I tried to save the situation. "This room is perfect," I said, and pointed to some equipment in the corner. "We can throw some colored light on that thing, and put the camera here, and it will look great." Patricia and Craig didn't look convinced.

Kevin was born and raised in the Bronx, and the veil of politeness was falling off his New York accent as he became more irritated. "So what do you want to do?" he asked finally, and with frustration in her voice, Pat agreed that we would just have to make it work.

Craig and Pat stayed behind while I walked with Kevin back down the hall to the first room he'd taken us to, to retrieve some equipment I'd left there.

"Sheesh," Kevin, said as we rounded the corner, out of their earshot. "You work with these morons every day?"

I said that I did.

"Yea, well, if I were you," he said, now in full Bronx voice, "I'd be polishing up my resume."

I thought about that in the van back to the station. I had spent months being treated like a misfit and feeling like a failure. It had never occured to me that the way they operated was lacking professionalism. With a new perspective, I booked a flight to Austin that very night.

A few weeks later I arrived in Texas with a backpack full of clothes and about a dozen pages of directions I'd printed from the internet, telling me how to take buses from the airport to my hostel, and to a couple of other supposedly hip areas around the city. It was the first time I'd flown in nearly a decade, and after landing, I cautiously followed the crowd off the plane and tried to make sense of airport signs like "ground transportation" and "shared ride vans." I found my bus without too much trouble, and I slung my backpack off my shoulders and through its door, and my body slipped in just as they closed; heading for downtown.

The bus dropped me off on Congress Avenue, and I walked a few blocks to get on a different bus that would take me across a bridge and within walking distance of my hostel. I caught that bus around the time school had let out, and it was full of latino middle school kids in matching uniforms, and they smiled with relief as they sipped cold sodas and snacked on bright orange wagon-wheel shaped pastries.

I took the last seat available, which was next to a young latina girl in a wrinkled polo blouse and a dark blue skirt. A cell phone rang in her backpack, and she took the cheap, pay-as-you-go device out to answer it.

"Bueno," she said, and paused to listen. "Si…"

She only spoke for a minute, and with my limited spanish, I was able to follow along: Yes, she was on the bus. Her day was fine. She would be home soon. Bye.

These were all experiences that were alien to me. I'd never been west of the Mississippi. I'd never been on a bus full of non-english speakers. And I'd never been this far from Maryland. As the bus crossed the

Congress street bridge over the Colorado river, it occured to me that this was all very out of character.

I checked into the hostel and left my bag in a small cubby beneath my bed. It was about 4 in the afternoon, and the room was hot and poorly ventilated. There were some people hanging out on a patio behind the building, so I walked out there to check it out. Outside, two guys sat on top of a picnic table, and rested their feet on the wooden bench. They each took long draws of cigarettes as they chatted, and looked at me suspiciously, like I was a boy scout.

I asked if they knew where I could find some live music, and they both said they didn't know the city very well. One was in town from Houston, interviewing for few jobs. The other was from Alabama, and here looking for his daughter, whose mother, he said, had violated their custody agreement and brought her to Austin to live with her new boyfriend. He was in town for a few days acting as his own PI, driving around to some spots where he thought they might be.

"Any luck?" I asked.

He exhaled a long stream of smoke and shook his head, then shrugged, casually, as if to say: *but what are you gonna do?*

I wished them both luck and turned to leave.

"6th Street," the man with the missing daughter said as I walked away. "Music is on 6th Street."

I walked back to the bus stop and eventually made my way to 6th Street, which was near where I had come from not long before. I noticed only now that the street was lined with nightclubs, but it was early, and they hadn't yet opened. I decided just to stroll for a while, and thus began what would be three days of walking nowhere in particular, by myself, while accomplishing very little.

The thing I remember most about that trip to Austin was that it was hot as hell. It was late September, and I'd packed appropriately for that season in Maryland; with jeans, a few t-shirts, and a light jacket to wear as I explored. As I began to walk that night on 6th Street it became obvious that this was an entirely different climate.

I spent the following days walking around the city with a rapidly deteriorating case of a condition commonly caused by sweat, and often referred to as "swamp ass." If you've never had swamp ass, imagine a scenario in which your butt cheeks have been adhered together with a strong glue, and the next step you take rips them apart, then quickly adheres them together again, only to be ripped apart again with the next step. Now imagine that for nine miles a day on hot urban pavement beneath the redneck fucking Texas sun.

The other thing I remember about that trip is being very lonely. If I were alone in a strange city today, I'd spend a good chunk of the day texting or communicating with friends through social media. Texting was a thing in 2008, but at that time in my life, I didn't really have anyone to text. I had friends of course, but none who knew I was in Texas or who would have cared to follow that saga particularly closely. I didn't like to open up to people, so no one would have known that I was miserable and in need of a major change.

So I walked. Past the clock tower from which Charles Whitman killed a dozen people with a sniper rifle in the '60s, and past the massive dome of the Texas capitol. Past countless music venues without entering a single one. I walked up and down Congress Avenue until the western sky was a vivid spectrum of pinks and blues. Then I walked down Guadalupe, where the college kids hung out, and I self-consciously wondered if every cute girl I saw could tell from my limp and the expression on my face that my butt cheeks felt like they had been sandblasted raw.

At the hostel at night, I hung out on the patio with the other transients and listen to them talk for a while before walking some more. The amateur detective hadn't yet found his daughter. The other guy had a few interviews and was feeling pretty good about one in particular. Another guy told me about a near fatal motorcycle accident he had been in a few years earlier, in which he'd broken nearly every bone in his body, and spent a year recovering in a body cast. "That sounds terrible," I said. *But have you ever had swamp ass?*

I walked from the hostel to South Congress for a beer, which turned into a few beers and some friendly chatting with a small group of strangers. I bought late-night barbeque from a place that glowed neon orange in the moonlit sky, and then walked back to the hostel, somewhat lost in the dark suburban sprawl. The neighborhood was built upon rocky soil, and tall cacti grew in the gardens of its comfortable homes. I licked smokey barbeque sauce off my fingers as I marched beside my shadow through the western darkness, and I knew that I wasn't going to move to Texas.

The Education Channel crew was standing around the window when I returned to work on Tuesday. John smirked and asked if I had "found myself," and I wondered why that was something older people get such a kick out of asking younger people.

That week at work, I had an assignment to webstream a training session for teachers. I had to take a camera, a laptop, and some other gear to a school and stream a classroom exercise to other schools around the county. It was an easy job, and all the equipment seemed to be working as I had tested it.

At some point during the session, a woman from the school system tapped me on the shoulder. "Can you follow the speaker," she whispered.

I looked at her with a puzzled expression, and pointed to the laptop, where my video feed was playing so I could monitor the quality. The speaker was centered in the frame, so I didn't know what she was talking about. When she saw that, she sat back down, satisfied.

A minute later, a gentleman came up to me with the same feedback. Again, I pointed to the monitor and whispered that everything looked fine on my end, and that the video it displayed was the same thing going out on the web.

After a moment, I felt the vibration of my cell phone in my pocket and without looking at the caller ID, I knew it was Jeff, the director of the Education Channel. He asked me to lock down my camera and step outside, and when I did, he chewed me out through the phone's receiver. *This was basic camera work,* he said. *How could I not know how to frame a shot,* he asked. *I was making the whole station look awful,* he told me.

Apparently, somewhere in the network, the video feed was compressing incorrectly. Viewers weren't seeing my whole camera shot, just a small portion of it. If you can imagine watching a football game on TV and seeing only the coaches standing on the sideline instead of players on the field, that's essentially what was happening. But while I was shooting, there was no way for me to know that, and there was no way to prove that the issue wasn't my own incompetence.

If I hadn't had twenty-thousand dollars worth of camera gear in my car to return, I probably would have just gone home. No two weeks. No goodbye. I'd have just turned off my phone and crawled into bed and slept for a few days, then re-emerged to begin looking for a new job.

I did go back, though. I wasn't fired on the spot. I asked Jeff if I should be worried, and he said "I think so," and sent me home for the weekend.

I managed to string a few more weeks together, but every day I wondered if the axe would fall, and I made more mistakes to bury myself deeper. John and Craig and Pat treated me like a ghost. Our watercooler talk shortened to nothing, as if their subconsciouses were telling them *I'd better not get too attached to this kid.*

If a superior ever calls you into a room in which you know he is alone by saying, "come see us please," you're probably about to be fired. That's what Jeff did one afternoon in late October. All day long I had been thinking, *I'm getting fired today,* and then, sure enough, it happened. Also know this: If you're paranoid you're getting fired, then you're getting fired.

Technically, Jeff didn't fire me. Instead, he sat me down and laid out my options. "It's a lot of paperwork with the county to have someone fired and it's a real pain," he explained. "But I'll do it."

I asked exactly what that meant.

"It means I expect you to resign," he said bluntly. "You can do it today or put in two weeks. I don't really care."

I thought for a moment about how much money I had in the bank, and said I'd put in my two weeks. I immediately wished I had told him to fuck off, but I guess you can't always be the hero you deserve.

I was grateful to have the extra paycheck before plunging back into unemployment. In the last two weeks, I went on a few more shoots and ironically, my footage was starting to turn around. I was beginning to get a hang of the gear they used and the way they wanted me to shoot. Maybe it was the pressure taken off me, or maybe I had just made every mistake there was to make, and those lessons were starting to yield results. Either way, it didn't really matter.

As my final day approached, it began to sink in that I had no plan. I had gone to Austin hoping to fall in love with it, and instead it just reiterated how alone I felt. For the first time since I was 16, there wasn't anything "next." Life could have been anything, but mostly it was looking like shit. I was a shit musician who shouldn't have quit his shit job, at which I was also shit, and which I now had to quit.

On my last day, I packed my things into a box. Everyone shook my hand and wished me luck. I said we'd keep in touch, but I knew we wouldn't. I stepped out of the brick building and into the autumn haze, and I knew that inside, John and the others had gathered in silence in the blue glow of the window to watch a grainy silhouette walk to its car.

# Modern Times

The first place I ever felt at home as a musician was an open mic in Washington, DC called Modern Times Open Mic. It was in a small coffee shop called Modern Times Coffee, which was in the basement of Politics and Prose; a popular book store that regularly hosted readings from authors, politicians, and poets. The events there had an inside-the-beltway leftward slant, and it was particularly popular amongst aging hippies and old money women from Bethesda, Chevy Chase, and other affluent neighborhoods in northwest DC.

That left-leaning audience may have been a reason for my comfort there. It was the summer of 2008, and I was writing angsty anti-Bush songs that gave way to angsty anti-Palin songs that gave way to hopeful, *Holy shit, I can't believe we actually elected Obama* songs. When I sang them at Modern Times, the old ladies would smile and clap in approval like proud grandmas, which helped me forget how horrifically I still sucked.

It was an acoustic open mic, which meant there was no sound system, and performers had to learn project with their voices. Since the room was small, I'd try to interact with the audience and make eye contact. If I sang a line I thought was funny, I'd laugh a little while singing to accent it. If a lyric was sad, I'd frown. The audience was generous, so I learned not just to play and sing, but to use subtle theatrics to bring the songs to life.

I began going to Modern Times sporadically in the summer of 2008, and became a regular in the fall after I had been fired from the Education Channel. When that job ended, I quickly started a temporary position my friend Annette had connected me with at the then-new Capitol Visitor Center on Capitol Hill, and was living in Annette's spare bedroom in Northern Virginia. On Friday nights I'd take the Metro from Capitol South to the Pentagon, a bus to Annette's house, change my clothes, then take my car back into DC and across town to the bookstore. I was new to the area and now know that I was taking one of the least efficient routes possible; but I almost always managed to make signup on time.

My contract at the Capitol Visitor Center was a beautiful example of government waste in action. The facility hadn't yet opened to the public, and was undergoing what they called a "Test and Adjust Phase". That meant on weekends, they invited members of the military and their families, government employees, and students to visit in advance of the grand opening and complete feedback surveys about their experience.

As you would expect in an inspiring new museum dedicated to the endurance of American democracy, the bulk of the feedback was about the food.

"The butternut squash soup was delicious," some people wrote. Or, "the cafeteria was lovely but a bit on the pricey side."

My job was to enter the results of these paper surveys into a computer and compile a report of the findings. I combed through hundreds of these comments each day, and entered them dutifully into a computer that sat in an information kiosk next to a statue of Astronaut John Swigert Jr. "The bread on the grilled cheese was under-browned," I typed over and over. The clacking of my mechanical keyboard echoed through the empty marble chamber.

When I had entered the last of the surveys into the system, I wrote a detailed report of the findings. There was no one supervising me, and I felt important to be in sole control of a final piece of a four-billion dollar facility that would endure for generations.

I put care into it like Thomas Jefferson writing the Declaration of Independence, laboring over every word - outlining the highlights and lowlights of visitor experience, and made a neatly bulleted list of ten low-cost recommendations for improvement.

I imagined bringing my kids to the Capitol someday, and showing off the mark I'd left on the place. "You know, kids: these bathrooms have clear signage because of your old man," I'd say with pride. "And my god, we MUST try the grilled cheese!"

When the report was completed I had it printed and bound in the Capitol's print shop, then delivered it to the desk of Beth Plemmons, the Visitor Center's director. I had learned to be intimidated by Beth from the way others spoke of her. She was an official in the Federal government, and the staff at the Capitol referred to her respectfully as "the director." Today, however, I wasn't intimidated. I was proud of my work, and confident she'd be impressed.

"Can I help you?" she asked after I had pushed my way into her office, report in hand.

"I'm just dropping off the ol' Test and Adjust Report," I said.

"The what?" she asked.

"The Test and Adjust Report," I repeated. "It's all the feedback from the preview visitors."

She stared at me stone-faced.

"It's what I've been working on for the last three months," I told her.

"Okay..." she said, trailing off with uncertainty. "I guess you can just put it in there." She gestured towards a wooden inbox that sat on the corner of her desk, that poured over with similar sized documents and loose pieces of paper. I knew immediately that she may as well have pointed to an incinerator.

I dropped it in the inbox and spun to walk out, and I could hear her resume typing as the door of her office closed behind me. As I walked through the hall of cubicles a grin spread across my face. I had just spent hours upon hours pouring a lot of heart into something that no one would ever care about. It was pretty good practice for being a folk singer, but at least this time I got paid.

At Modern Times, people at seemed to care about my writing. The host was Maureen Nelson, who liked my music and soon became a close friend. Other regulars included my future roommates Adrian Krygowski and Ken Wenzel, Bass player Hess Muse, blues singer Denise Buck (aka Papa Denny), keyboard player Ian Walters, instrumental group StarFKRadium, and singer songwriters Rene Moffat, Jay Paslay, and Joe Harris.

After the open mic we'd stand in the parking lot jamming, and eventually migrate over to Comet Ping Pong for late night beers and pizza. We couldn't have known at the time that Comet Ping Pong would one day be known for "PizzaGate," a right wing conspiracy theory about how the democratic party was running a child sex trafficking ring from its nonexistent basement. In those days, we just knew it for having a kitchen that was open late.

It felt good to have a community in my new city. I was still recovering emotionally from my experience at the Education Channel, and I was starting to remember that under the right circumstances, people actually like me.

It was in these first few months in DC that I met Jamee. It was the first day back at work at the Capitol after New Years Day, and I emerged from the Capitol South metro station to find it was raining. It hadn't been raining when I'd left Fairfax, so I didn't have an umbrella. I approached the Capitol's security line in the cold January morning, expecting to spend the next five to ten minutes developing a case of pneumonia.

Near me, in the back of the line, I noticed a cute girl holding an extra large umbrella, andI decided to go for it.

"Excuse me," I asked. "Do you mind if I stand with you?"

She said I could, and after talking in line for a few minutes we agreed to meet up later. She was just in town for a month as an intern and like me, didn't know know very many people. I had the Modern Times crew, but we were still in the early stages of friendship where I only saw them on Fridays at the open mic itself.

Jamee and I started hanging out and the rest is history. She helped me move into the first room I ever rented. She came to Modern Times with me and hung out afterwards at Comet with my musician friends. It wasn't romantic at first; she was more like my little buddy. The fact that I had been in town for two months longer than her made me feel like I knew my way around, and her ability to go with the flow helped me feel less embarrassed when I reliably proved I didn't.

One day at work, I was given a package by the director to deliver to another office in the Capitol complex, numbered B222. I texted Jamee to see if she wanted to come, and she said she could probably slip out of her intern duties for a few minutes.

B222, I was told, should mean "Basement level 2, office 22" but we could find no such room. We found B221 and B223, but there was nothing in between them. We stopped to ask a few guards, and no one could give us any helpful ideas. We wandered around for a few hours, riding the underground trams between the buildings in the Capitol, laughing at all the young, suit-clad congressional staffers thumbing their Blackberrys, who seemed to be taking themselves very seriously.

Later, I dropped the package back off with Beth and told her I couldn't find the office. She shrugged, and put it back into a pile with other misfit documents.

Jamee left to study abroad in Peru in early February and left me on my own again, but having her around for the month helped me make friends and I felt I was in a much better place when she left. We agreed to keep in touch and see if we could make things work long distance, and they did.

In January I had finished a song called "Dry Town," and it had made a name for me in the DC acoustic scene. "Dry Town Brad" they called me. People would start singing it when I walked into the room. Thanks to "Dry Town", I started to play showcases at small venues, which helped me meet more musicians.

In DC, a "showcase" wasn't that big of a deal. It usually meant playing through a cheap PA to an unwitting audience at a dive bar or Ethiopian restaurant, but since you had to be invited to play them, it was cooler to be invited than not to be. I was still very amatuer, and it was validating to break out of open mics and earn opportunities to play longer sets - sometimes even with my name printed on paper fliers that we'd hand out on the street before the show. I loved doing all of that. It made me feel like we were in the village in the sixties, hustling, trying to be heard.

I rented a tiny room in Silver Spring just outside DC from a guy named Neel Singh who I met through craigslist, but it turned out we had a few mutual friends. Neil was a guitar player in a band called Drop Electric, and a great resource when I was working on music. He liked to party and there were always people in the house. I'd come home from work to find three guys passed out surrounded by beer cans after a long after afternoon of weekday day-drinking.

One day in late February I reported to work at the Capitol Visitor Center and grew concerned when people seemed surprised to see me there. A woman named Shelly delicately advised me to call the company that was administering my temp contract. I called, and learned that there apparently had been some confusion about the duration of my employment; most notably about the fact that it ended the previous day. I was sent home and once again, had nothing lined up for work.

I fell into the familiar pattern that I had been in before I began at the Education Channel. I'd interview for jobs and be passed over, but recommended to someone else who might have an opening. One day I interviewed for a position as an events manager at an auditorium at the George Washington University. I didn't get the job, but they liked me enough to keep me as a contractor. This would become the main source of the meager income I'd be able to stitch together for the next year and a half.

George Washington wound up being a decent place to work. The venue hosted political speakers, conferences, and performances. There, I got to meet John Kerry, Jeb Bush, Larry King, David Gregory, John Lewis, Ira Glass, Thomas Friedman, and many others. These interactions usually came as I put microphones on them and ask them if they needed a beverage.

Some events at GW were just a few hours long, and others were conferences that required me to be there from 5am until nearly midnight for days in a row. As a part of a small team, these exhausting hours brought us close together. I became friends with Jason Moore, who had beat me out for the full time job. He was also a musician, and we liked to sit in the control booth and make fun of the conference speakers. The stage manager was Lily, and she was so responsible and on top of things that I couldn't believe it when I found out she was actually a few years younger than me - barely 22.

The director of the entire facility was a woman named Maureen Ryan. She was single and didn't have kids, and I think she truly loved the three of us and the dynamic of our team. There were events where I definitely wasn't needed, but she'd build my hours into quotes because she knew I needed the work.

Sometimes there were no events at the auditorium for weeks at a time, and during these stretches Maureen would occasionally hire me for a few hours here and there to inventory or maintain equipment, or just to come in and move lights around the auditorium's grid for no real reason. I suspected these were make-work projects for me, but I was broke enough to happily accept them.

She also helped me find other contract gigs. One of these was a similar job at the National Press Club, where again, I'd enjoy chance run-ins with the famous and influential. Once while setting up mics, I had a nice conversations with writers Dave Barry and Amy Tan, who were preparing for a press conference there - though I didn't know it was them until after I'd left their presence. The Press Club had multiple events going on at once almost every day, and I got to drop in on speeches by Sully Sullenberger, Condoleezza Rice, and Dick Cheney, among others.

The best thing about the Press Club was the food. It was a high-end venue, and the kitchen kept a generous buffet available for the staff. I got into the practice of bringing tupperware and stocking up, and as a result, sometimes theirs was the only food I ate for days at a time.

The worst thing about the Press Club was the people who worked there fell on the miserable side of the spectrum. Running 20 events per day is not an easy job, and I think my supervisor handled the pressure the way anyone would: with a healthy amount of cocaine. It wasn't uncommon for him to disappear into his office for a few minutes, then come out sniffling but very excited for the panel discussion on African agricultural capacity building in Room 4.

These jobs helped me stitch together an income, but I still had no health insurance. One day in the fall of 2009, I worked a shift from 6 pm until midnight at GW, and again the next day from 5 am until 1 pm at the Press Club. When I got home, I climbed into bed, and awoke the following day at 7pm, after nearly 30 hours of sleep. My roommates told me they had argued for a while over who would enter my room and make sure I was still alive, and when one of them had the courage to check my pulse, they were relieved to learn I hadn't died in my sleep.

I had no energy for days after that, and with financial help from my mom, went to the doctor and was diagnosed with mono. I spent the following few weeks on my parent's couch in Virginia, watching TV action-dramas from the eighties on cable, devastated about all the work I had to cancel.

As I was starting to get better, I heard of an opening at the 16th Street Music House, just a few miles away from the Silver Spring house where I'd been living. The 16th street house was a large, brick home in DC's Brightwood neighborhood rented by several folk musicians. Adrian Krygowski and Ken Wenzel were Modern Times regulars, and Maureen Andary was another folk singer I knew from playing showcases around town. There was also Jason Chmiola, a recording engineer who worked on staff at a local studio. Maureen's boyfriend, Johnny Grave, was a phenomenal blues guitarist and singer and essentially the 6th resident of the house. There were a handful of bands that rehearsed there, and they also had shows in the basement.

When I heard of that opening, I grabbed it. I wanted to be around the creative energy of other folk singers. I also had heard that Jason was the kind of guy who liked to help folk singers make records, so I wanted to get to know him better.

It ended up being a great decision, and I matured as a writer living there. I learned a lot from watching Adrian and Maureen work, arranging songs over and over until they felt just right.

Jason and I wound up hitting it off pretty quickly. It was often just the two of us in the house, and we'd grill sausages and watch police chase shows while I'd strum my guitar. Once a week, we'd go to half-price burger night nearby at the Quarry House. I told him one day in the spring of 2010 that I was thinking I'd like to make a record, and he said he'd be happy to help out.

The only thing I really knew about the record I wanted to make was that it was going to be called "Fear and Drought." I didn't actually have a song called "Fear and Drought" yet, but I knew that I would write it and it would be the title track. I had decided this around the time I started playing guitar, when I found the words "The only things we have to fear are fear itself and drought," doodled on a page in a notebook from college as I was cleaning one day. I liked the way it sounded, and I knew when I saw it that it was going to be a song.

Jason and I mapped out some logistics for the project and decided we would start recording in early May. I had never made a record before, and I enjoyed the process of breaking down my songs, and trying to decide how to arrange them. I took some recordings I liked to Jason and we'd talk about how to recreate the sound. I was obsessed with the way Bob Dylan layered organ and piano in a chaotic arrangement in songs like "Sooner or Later,"and I loved the honkey tonk piano layered with violin in Wilco's "Dreamer in my Dreams." These songs became the biggest inspiration for the production.

Adrian connected me with a drummer named Mike Smirnoff, and when we got together to practice, it became clear that he was more than a brilliant percussionist, but also helping me produce the album by introducing dynamics, and helping me flesh out the tempo of the record. These were things I'd never thought of, and his skill made the whole project possible. We practiced in the basement of the 16th street house, and Mike's discipline helped ensure that when I got to the studio, I knew exactly what I wanted each song to sound like. Mike was the biggest line item in my record's budget, but his help with preparation paid for itself many times over.

As May approached, I still didn't have a song called "Fear and Drought." The record depended on it. One day I was working a video editing job when I took a break to wait for my computer to render some edits. I had a pad of paper in front of me, and I wrote the words "Fear and Drought" at the top. Ten minutes later it was done. It flowed out of me with an ease I had never experienced before. I took the lyrics home and set it to music just as quickly. I played it for Jonny Grave and he said, "you just wrote that now?" I thought that was a good sign, and he agreed to play steel guitar for it on my record.

Another song I wrote just before we went into the studio was called "Mount St. Helens." I'd been playing with the guitar riff for a few months and I'd had the line, "waiting for the flowers on Mount St. Helens to bloom," in my head for a few years. It didn't occur to me they fit together until I was buying a coke at a convenience store near GW one day, and I saw that Mount St. Helens was the cover story on that month's issue of National Geographic. It clicked in my mind, and I went home and wrote the lyrics in a couple of hours.

Jamee was about to graduate college and had been offered a position in California. She'd decided that she was going to move, and I hadn't yet decided if I would.

That changed one night on the steps outside my building at GW, when I was going in late to use their editing suites for a video job they'd hired me for. I had a cup of coffee in my hand, and a few different bags of gear draped over my shoulders. It was a delicate balance, and my hand shook as I reached out to touch my RFID to the door and pull it open. I grabbed the door's handle with the outstretched fingers of the same hand that was holding my coffee and when I twisted it to open the door, I very stupidly poured the coffee all over myself.

I was immediately filled with a deep sense of self-hatred and came very close to causing a scene. I let the bags slide off my shoulders and onto the ground, and spiked the coffee cup onto the concrete.I sat on the steps and cursed myself for a few minutes before I calmed down and scanned the empty street.

"I don't really have a lot going for me here, do I?" I finally said aloud. "I should just fucking go to California." It was a big decision in my life, and one that put a new sense of urgency on finishing my record.

In May, we started working at Jason's studio late at night when he could use it without his boss finding out he was underbilling hours upon hours of time to friends. The studio was magical to me, but also a challenge to my confidence. It didn't take long to learn that professional studio microphones are not as warm an audience as the old ladies at Modern Times.

This was the spring of 2010 and I'd only been singing since the summer of 2007. It was unrealistic to expect my voice to sound like the ones on the records I'd grown up listening to, but it was still damning to hear it played back on the high resolution studio monitors. But Jason was patient and a technical wizard, and using a combination of on-the-fly voice coaching, different microphones, and EQ and reverb settings, we were able to get the vocals to a point I was comfortable with.

In fact, my voice is the only thing about the record I don't love. With guitar by Jonny Grave, Adrian, and Neel, Mike's drums, bass by Jason, piano from Ian Walters, and amazing violin from Alan Oresky (who I found on Craigslist) the production sounds incredible. Jason would send me playbacks during the day, and I'd struggle to contain my excitement.

The sessions were spread out over several months, which gave me time to make some important decisions about each song. When the bulk of the recording was nearly done, I still felt like something was missing from Mount St. Helens.

I was at Modern Times thinking about it one night when a guy got on stage with an instrument I'd never seen before. It was a broad, flat stick with 10 strings, and it slung over his shoulder from a strap like a guitar. It was electric, and a small amp sat beside him on the floor. He said his name was Flint Blade, and he was visiting from Florida. His instrument, he said, was called a chapman stick. When he started playing, I knew immediately that I wanted it on Mount St. Helens.

I called Jason on my phone while Flint was playing and asked if he could get his small studio in our basement fired up in the next hour. He asked why, and I held up the phone. He told me he could make it happen.

When Flint got off stage, I asked if he'd want to come back to our house and play on a record. He said he was on vacation with parents, "so hell yea."

In our basement, it took him just a couple of takes to nail Mount St. Helens. He tapped the strings of the chapman stick delicately, and layed down a texture that was simple and ethereal. I listened through Jason's headphones, and knew I was hearing the pure magic that is music; a chance encounter between two strangers, the shared spirit of creativity, and the creation of something enduring and beautiful.

If there are an infinite number of universes, then there are an infinite number in which I didn't meet Flint Blade and his chapman stick that Friday night; but I'm glad I live in this one.

As the Summer was winding down so was my time in DC. At GW, Maureen Ryan had been let go, and with her, my work there ended. Jamee had moved to California and I was planning my trip out to join her in October. I was working an increasing number of terrible one-off gigs to make money in the meantime. But mostly, I was focused on the record.

We were running out of time and in preparation for my move, I was getting stingier with money. I decided I needed to cut the album from eleven tracks to nine, and that two of those would be acoustic.

In September, I got a job offer in California. I had been looking in DC for two years with nothing but rejection. California was starting to look like the land of milk and honey.

In a way, completing the album was anticlimactic. We'd been piecing it together for so long that I was ready for it to be over. I performed "Churchill's Greatest Speech" for Jason at the studio late one night, and called it. "Churchill" wasn't as good as I wanted it to be, but only because it was an accurate representation of how I sounded.

Jason would spend the some time during month after I left DC mixing the album and completing it. When he had a new mix, he'd email it to me across the country.

The night before I moved I had a going away party. It began where it all started back at Modern Times. Maureen Nelson let me be the featured artist that night, and then we all migrated back to my house for a blowout party. Friends from high school and college came, but the most dominant force at the party were the folks from DC, especially my roommates at the 16th street house. There are photographs of me standing on our couch playing music. There were a lot of shots. I woke up with a red, white, and blue capo in my pocket, and to this day I don't know where it came from.

I wasn't the first person to leave the 16th Street house a disaster, or I would have felt worse about it. I left early the next morning and rolled out to Virginia, where I'd stay with my parents for a few days before heading to California. When I drove across the country, it all felt like a dream: two years of my life marked mostly by struggling to get by; with no career or money to show for it - but I had a record I was proud of that no one could take from me.

There have been countless records that have been important to me and have defined phases of my life; from Bowie's "Ziggy Stardust" to the Rolling Stones, "Exile on Main Street." I left DC with one I had made myself; an accidental concept album that documented both what I was feeling during those two years and the talent of the people I was with. I had rebuilt myself from a traumatic experience, found love, and made life-long friends. Driving through the southwest, they were all 2,000 miles behind me. But when I popped Jason's early mixes of "Fear and Drought" into my car's CD player, I knew that as long as I had my guitar and a place to play, I'd never really be alone again.

# *Keep on Keeping On*

From ages five to fourteen I played youth soccer through a local organization called the Westminster Optimist Soccer League, with the operative word in that title being "optimist." *Could we be professional soccer players one day, coach?* That's optimistic. In fact, most of us left our air conditioned homes only at the insistence of our parents, who in most cases, registered us for the league to mitigate our risk of juvenile bedsores.

The Optimist League was a safe place for the physically unfit and athletically disinterested. My dad coached our team, and we had a kid who went by "Loaf," and a pair of effeminate brothers who'd chase the ball around the field while belting show tunes. Another kid had Down Syndrome, and when an opposing player scored against us, he'd tackle them to the ground for a joyous celebration hug. Then there was our secret weapon: a pock-faced early blooming girl, who at 8 feet tall, would tear down the pitch and distract male defenders with her mature, bouncing tits.

Though I wasn't particularly competitive, I was one of the better players in the league. At 13 years old I was a sleek 80 pounds, which made me fast and maneuverable. With the benefit of a soccer clinic my parents had sent me to, I could dazzle the league with fancy footwork; stealing the ball from an opponent, faking to the left, then to the right, then backwards, then forward - straight through their legs. It was my one trick, but it worked against my meager Optimist League opponents so well that after one game, the opposing coach approached me.

"You're good," he said, and I thanked him. "My other son plays on a club team," he continued. "I can get you a tryout, if you want." I was flattered to be asked, and my parents were happy to take me to the high school one night later that week to tryout - though I didn't really know what that entailed.

When I arrived at their practice, the kids on the club team were wearing Adidas warm up suits and standing in a tight circle, passing a soccer ball around in the air using only their knees and heads. Occasionally, someone would let the ball fall behind him, then kick it back into the circle with his heel before it touched the ground. These kids were lean and muscular like greyhounds, and much bigger than me: at least average size for someone my age. Their coach told me to go join them and warm up, and my plastic shin guards slapped against my legs as I jogged over.

Most of what happened in the hour that followed is a blur, but I do know I left the tryout spiritually neutered by an animal-like sense of defeat. For several months I had an aversion to my own reflection, and was prone to long walks alone in the woods, where I'd dig what I now recognize were "shame holes."

The other kids had done things with a soccer ball that I didn't know were possible. They easily deflected my "fake out" trick, and then passed the ball between each other in the air, using what I still believe was a form of demonic telekinesis.

When I climbed back into the car, my mom asked how I thought it went, and I looked straight ahead without expression. "Just drive," I said, and I went to great lengths for the remainder of my youth to avoid, under any circumstance, seeing any of those kids again.

In 2010, I moved from Washington, DC to San Francisco, and knew that feeling all over. In DC, I had steadily been moving up the ranks on the folk scene. I'd only been playing music for 2 years, but my songs were getting better. I could get a band together when I needed to, and we could put on a decent show in a number of legitimate venues. I was still very green, but the talent pool was small, and I was beginning to develop a level of polish that helped me stand out.

In San Francisco, this was not the case. There were more singer-songwriters, and many of them were writing and performing at a professional level. Some I'd find out had long musical careers, and had even flirted with fame. Others had publishing deals, with singles placed in movies or TV shows. The baseline of talent was much higher, so on the rare occasion I'd get booked anywhere, I'd sit through the other acts with a deep sense of dread, awaiting my turn to take the stage and embarrass myself.

I released my album, "Fear and Drought" in February of 2011, and it exacerbated my fears of irrelevance. I don't know how many people bought it, but I'd carry a box on unsold copies with me for years. The few reviews I got were written by very nice people who were clearly not that into the music. The world was confirming my fears that I'd started too late, and had no talent. I also hadn't finished a song in months, and I was feeling stale.

It had been about 3 years since I'd heard "Love Minus Zero" and decided I could write my own songs. Since then, I learned the instrument, learned to sing, written about thirty songs, made an album, and played dozens of shows. I had exceeded my own expectations, and now found myself on a plateau, struggling to find a foothold to the next level. *Maybe, this thing has run its course,* I thought, and tried to convince myself that I was okay with that.

One night I saw that alt-country singer Elizabeth Cook was coming to San Francisco to play a show at the Great American Music Hall. I had seen Elizabeth once before, and I knew my friend Andy from Baltimore had managed her for a while. My mom was visiting, and I thought she and Jamee would enjoy Elizabeth's music. I shot Andy a text to see if he could hook me up with free tickets.

Andy texted me back before long, and told me there were tickets for us on the guest list. Elizabeth was the opening act supporting someone I'd never heard of, so I figured we'd watch her set, then leave early and get some dinner.

Elizabeth only played a short set that night, and we watched from the Balcony. When she was done, we decided we'd check out a song or two from the headlining act before leaving to get food.

When the lights in the old theatre went dark again, a slender, barefoot man took the stage. He slid the strap of a black acoustic guitar over his head and rested it on his shoulder. The crowd erupted in applause at the sight of him, and a half dozen lighters flickered in the dark room, followed by streams of green smoke that wafted towards the ceiling.

The man wore an orange button down shirt, vest, and a brown felt hat. He scanned the room with a mischievous grin for a moment before gently flicking his guitar strings with his pick, and leaning in towards the mic. This was the first moment I had ever seen or heard Todd Snider, but by the time his first song ended, he was my favorite songwriter of all time. He opened with a song called "Greencastle Blues," and when he sang the line *How do you know when it's too late to learn,* it cut right to my heart.

It's not hyperbolic to say that Todd changed my life. Before I discovered him that night in San Francisco, I was about to quit music because I didn't think I was a good enough at singing or playing the guitar. Todd wasn't extremely good at either of those things in 2011, and yet there he was, playing for 300 fans who knew the words to every song. Between songs, he told self-deprecating stories - sometimes about how he wasn't a great singer or great guitar player, and that made people loved him even more.

Todd was no clown, though. His songs were masterfully crafted and rich with brilliant wordplay and layers of meaning, and he cranked out great ones - one after another - all night long. When he started taking requests, conflicting ones rang out from across the room. *How many more great songs could this guy possibly have?* I wondered, and in the following weeks as I dove into his catalogue, it seemed like the list went on forever.

From his live record, "The Storyteller", I could study how he crafted stories to go along with each of his songs. Most musicians banter on stage to tell a story about how they got ideas for their songs, which I've always found painful. Todd's stories were part of the show itself; funny, surprising, and artfully delivered. They weren't necessarily about the songs, but served as a comic supplement to the song's sentiment, and through the pairing of songs and story, he sent the audience through a wide range of emotions.

The thing about Todd that inspired me the most was his confidence. He knew he wasn't the best musician, but he made no apologies on stage. He'd mess up a guitar lick, and the crowd would laugh with him. He'd flub a line, and he'd grin, and just keep going. In his self-deprecating style, it was all par for the course. The fact that his songs were world class helped with his confidence, I'm sure, as did the fact that he was playing to a room full of people who clearly adored him. He had a charisma that seemed to embrace being a fuck up, and in a room full of other fuck ups, he had them eating from the palm of his hand.

Before I discovered Todd, the personas who most heavily influenced me on stage were Julian Casablancas of The Strokes, and Bob Dylan. Those are two performers who take the stage, sing their songs, and don't banter or talk at all during their set. Since I'd seen so many cringe-worthy performers fumbling through awkward stories and bad jokes, I thought that was the right thing to do. I'd play one song, pause for a moment, and jump into the next. Todd made me rethink everything. For the second time in my life as a musician, those delusional words flashed in my mind. *I could probably do that.*

When you're an artist and you have influences, one of the biggest fears you have is being accused of ripping someone off. Even worse is being accused of trying to *be* that person, because the older you get, the more embarrassing it is to be caught by your peers living in a fantasy.

I've found the only way to deal with this is to just do it - time and time again. If your goal is to be original, you'll eventually beat the impersonation out of yourself through repetition, gradually uncovering more and more of your own style each time. Jerry Garcia said "You can't avoid finding your own voice if you keep playing. You have a voice, whether you recognize it or not," and I agree.

Bob Dylan's early Woody Guthrie impression ultimately evolved into his own brilliance. The American rock and roll sound of the Beatles eventually turned into their own thing. If you're afraid to do something because you're too similar to someone else, my advice is to keep doing it until you're not.

With an on-stage storytelling persona, that's basically what I did. If you'd seen me perform the first year I was into Todd, you'd have thought, *this guy's trying to be Todd Snider.*

It turned out it wasn't an easy feat. Todd says he can ramble on for 18 minutes between songs. I'd tell a story for what I was sure was 5 minutes, then listen to the playback and discover it was barely 45 seconds. I dug through my mind for interesting stories, and realized I didn't have a ton of them. By performing over and over, I got a sense of which parts of each story worked, and could find ways to embellish them, patch others together, or make new ones up entirely. As I did that, it occured to me that's probably pretty normal, and I abandoned the feeling of dishonesty that accompanied telling fake stories on stage, and instead focused on selling them.

It's my opinion that the thing we call "charisma" is the art of making strangers think they already know and like you. If you walk on stage and act like the audience knows they're in for a treat, you might just convince them they actually are. You don't need to introduce yourself or your songs; you just need to make everyone in the audience think they're the only one in the room that doesn't know them already.

Today, when I perform, people tell me I'm polished and confident. In reality, I'm neither of those things. I act like I am, and let people fulfill their own prophecy of enjoying it. I suppose that's a fancy way of saying "fake it 'til you make it," only, technically, I've never made it.

What I have made is a comfort level with myself that's always teetering on the brink of paranoia. *Sure I haven't made it,* I think. *But people seem to like me.* With the occasional add on, *but maybe they're just being polite.*

I call myself "semi-retired" because I don't shop myself around as an artist very often. I don't keep an email list or maintain a website, and I rarely proactively email bookers. A handful of times each year I get invited to play someplace by someone who has seen me before, which is validating. On the other hand, the phone isn't exactly ringing off the hook.

It's in this duet of confidence and doubt that I live as an artist, and I would suspect most singer/songwriters I know also exist on that spectrum. In fact, I would argue that every artist is completely crazy; trying to find a happy balance between the confidence that tells us we've got something the world needs to hear, and the doubt that tells us we're terrible or average, though I'm not sure which is worse.

I've made two records that no one bought. I've been passed over for every festival I've submitted myself for. At times, I can barely book a show in a coffee shop. All signs in my head should point to my arriving at the conclusion that I'm not a very appealing musician. Instead, my brain tells me *maybe if I just marketed myself better…* It's pure insanity.

In the fall of 2015 Todd Snider put a message on facebook saying that he was retiring from touring because of his chronic arthritis pain. My interpretation was far worse. I had read he was struggling with opiate addiction that summer, and had even seen him limp off stage in Santa Cruz with the help of his tour manager just months before. I thought he was dying and the announcement was his way of trying to say goodbye to his fans. I bought tickets for Jamee and I to see him one last time in Houston, Texas.

More than see his show, I wanted to meet him. He had been doing pre-show hangouts in parking lots with fans that tour, and I'd hoped if I got there early, he may come out out of his bus.

We arrived in Houston early after a dawn flight out of San Francisco, and drove our rental car to the venue. The place was called Main Street Crossing, and it was a small brick building on a potholed main street of a town called Tomball. It's always weird to see that someone you consider a national treasure and living legend is playing in a venue no larger than an Applebees, but that's the way it goes in folk music: even at the highest levels, it's not very popular.

We pulled up around 3:30pm, shortly after Todd's tour bus had arrived. I know this because we were greeted by a man who introduced himself as David Baker, who stood alone in the parking lot by his truck waving a flag with Todd's gypsy wheel logo. David was fifty, at least, and was shaking with excitement. This guy was the biggest Todd Snider fan in the world, without a doubt.

David had all the intel. The bus had just pulled up, he said, and Todd's tour manager said Todd was resting a bit, then would sound check, then might come out.

My friend Doug had a habit when he was a kid that he used to do when he was excited. He'd beat his arms up and down so it looked like he was flapping his wings like a bird. We called it "flapping," and it usually occurred in the moment of anticipation before we'd detonate something we weren't supposed to detonate with an accelerant we weren't supposed to possess. I mention that now because that's what David Baker was doing in the parking lot: showing an uncontainable amount of excitement about getting to meet Todd again.

I had taken my guitar with me to Tomball, and I took it out and sat on the tailgate of David's truck and played a few songs. Jamee, myself, and David hung out and chatted that way for a few minutes.

"Here he comes," David said, and leapt forward.

I looked up, and Todd was walking across the parking lot towards us. He was carrying a banjo and strumming it with his fingers as he walked. I could tell from his eyes and the way he walked that he was medicated. Up close, he was tall and muscular.

He said he had recognized David from the window of the bus, and wanted to come and say hi. He shook all of our hands, and stood there plucking his banjo as he talked to us for the next 20 minutes or so.

I asked if I could play a song for him, and he said of course, so I played "Dry Town," and he listened intently. When I sang the line, "we walk side by side, but we travel alone," he got excited.

"Nice!" he said. He told me he bet people sang along when I played that song, and I said sometimes they did. He asked if I was touring or trying to make it as a musician and I told him not really.

"That's okay," he said. "You know, the thing no one tells you is that a lot of it's luck."

I looked around the nearly empty parking lot and wondered if Todd considered himself someone who had made it. Here he was, talking to three of his fans in an otherwise empty lot as cars whizzed by on the street. If their occupants had noticed him at all, they would have seen a stoned looking man in dirty clothes, and had no idea that he meant so much to so many people.

Todd hung out with us for a little longer and posed for a few pictures. I gave him a capo I had gotten engraved with a Bob Dylan lyric, "the only thing I knew how to do was keep on keeping on." When he said he had to go rest up, I made him promise not to die on us. In this case, "us" meant "me."

During the show that night, his discomfort was obvious. He started a few songs without finishing them, and attempted to play his album, "East Nashville Skyline," in its entirety but couldn't remember the words to a few songs. He played for just a little over an hour, and his tour manager whisked him off stage, through the room and back to the bus. On the way home, Jamee and I were worried.

Of all the memories of being a musician, playing for Todd in that parking lot is my favorite. I still think a lot about what he told me that day about a lot of it being luck.

Today, I take "luck" to mean a lot of things. It might mean you get lucky at a gig and the right person hears you and can help with your career. You're lucky if five people like your music enough to show up to listen to you. At a more fundamental level, if what you love to do lines up with what you have a natural talent for, I think you're really lucky.

Part of me thinks calling it "luck" is a cop out: a lazy man's way of saying, "your dream didn't come true because you didn't get lucky." I never said I wasn't delusional, right?

If I hadn't taken a Bob Dylan class in college, I may have never heard "Love Minus Zero," which means I never would have thought I could be a musician. If I hadn't been fired from the Education Channel a year later, I never would have moved to DC which means I never would have met Jamee which means I never would have moved to California which means I wouldn't have my career or life here.

You can trace most of the phases in your life backwards to a single event that defines that phase, perhaps even an entire decade. The question is: do you want to? The fragility of it all is mind boggling, sometimes enough so to induce panic attacks.

If you're thinking about trying something new, I hope you'll keep in mind that the variables within your control will always pale in comparison to those outside of it. But if you work hard and say "yes" enough times, you may find yourself with more luck than if you don't.

Today I'm happy to report that Todd is still alive as of this writing and looking much better than he was in 2015. He's gotten stronger and is even playing shows standing up again. I've gotten to see him about 10 times since then, and he looks better and stronger each time.

As for me, I'm performing more frequently than I have in years and they are the kinds of shows I've dreamt of playing since I first started writing. My repertoire of songs has gotten strong enough that I feel I deserve the audiences I've gotten to play for, and my storytelling has evolved from a bad Todd Snider impression into a thing of my own.

While I haven't "made it," I always come off stage feeling like I found some of that luck Todd told me about in Texas in the fall of 2015. It's a feeling I hope to maintain through future phases of my semi-retirement, but I also know now to embrace the doubt when it comes and let it run its course. Ultimately, it's the only thing that keeps an artist from getting lost in delusion, and ensures we keep pushing ourselves to be better.

### Soldier of Fortune
### 2007

Soldier of fortune don't
look out your window
A sparrow is watching you
sleep like an angel
So put your head back down
On that old down pillow
just turn it back over to
the cool side again.
It's been warming all night
under all that brown hair
and toasting with kings
in your dreams.
So disregard screams
from the birds and go back to sleep.

Soldier of fortune don't
Wait for me walking.
The stranger I'm talking to
Thinks that you've fallen.
Hide and lay low and for
Comfort start rocking
You'll soon find a groove
You can live in again

It's hard to toss yourself
To the side like they did
I've done it before
so I know
Just hide down below
for or a while
and things will look up

Soldier of fortune don't
Hype up your worries
The blizzard they call for
May only be flurries
So don't mind the verdicts
you hear from the juries
they're biased and you know it
so just worry about yourself
The world seems against you
and the world seems so big
and the weight on your

Shoulders, it hurts.
Just go back to work
on good things
they'll need you again.

**Reception**
*2007*

When you're lost at sea for any length of time
And you're not sure if the sun is setting on your life
Don't be afraid to call me on the phone
As long as you have reception

When you are a drift and the winds begin to shift
And you're not sure if every minute is a gift
Or a curse or worse then to failure you are prone
Unless you have got some reception

No man can foresee what he can not imagine
So don't go out to sea without a traveled captain
If he jumps the ship then it's known he sets the tone
And I hope that you have reception

All those little dots are ships dragging knots
And the sailors are asleep in their cots
They're drifting out of port and they're dreaming all alone
And I bet that they have some reception

It's been said that Jesus saves but its waves that rock the boat
And the rowers are all slaves it's important to note
Their bodies are for keeps but their souls are just on loan
And I know that they have some reception.

Out here on the sea it means nothing to be free
if you can't read a map then you have no liberty
you have to know the stars or you'll never make it home
so I hope that you have some reception.

## Dry Town
## 2008

Dry Town, Dry Town
What a sad place I've found
I'm leaving tomorrow
I can't stick around

Dry Town, Dry Town,
No I can't stick around
I've got too much sorrow
That I need to drown

When the sun it was orange
And the air it was hot
I thought about the things that
I knew you forgot
You forgot all our seasons
You forgot all our years
And left me with nothing
To drink but my tears

When the cacti were green
And the road was made of dirt
I thought of the times that
you walked away hurt
We're silent like children
And though we are grown
We walk side by side
But we travel alone.

The most broken man
That ever I met
Came in your life
before me I bet
He asks for a drink
his mouth won't make sound
His throat must be dried out
Like this goddamn town

Dry Town, Dry Town
What a sad place I've found
I'm leaving tomorrow
I can't stick around

Dry Town, Dry Town,
I can't stick around
I've got too much sorrow
That I need to drown

### Fear and Drought
### *2010*

I'm walking down the back roads of this county
I'm sometimes known to look the other way
congressmen and convicts surround me
I don't trust a damn word that they say

I always hoped you'd be the one to tell me
there is no promised land on down the road
the promised land it seems
is just a product of our dreams
salvation isn't something that we're owed

Forgive me if I'm talkin' like I've got it figured out
The only thing we have to fear is fear itself and drought.

Every day I live feels like a Friday
I tried to grow up once, it didn't take
this gravel road, it used to be a highway
This puddle at my feet was once a lake

The sky sometimes looks like it's falling
that's just an illusion of the stars
You cannot make revisions
to your life's hardest decisions
sometimes only time can heal your scars

Forgive me if I'm talkin' like I've got it figured out
The only thing we have to fear is fear itself and drought.

I'm throwing heavy stones in the pacific

*trying to shift this land further west*
*endurance is the only way I'm gifted*
*survival is the game at which I'm best*

*I win a bet every time I wake up*
*I gamble every time I go to sleep*
*and if you play the cards you're dealt*
*you'll never have to starve yourself*
*the wealth of kings will be yours to keep*

*Forgive me if I'm talkin' like I've got it figured out*
*The only thing we have to fear is fear itself and drought*

### Mount St. Helens
### 2010

*I hope I'll be notified*
*When you decide*
*that you on your way*
*out the door*
*to look for more*
*and what's in store*
*you cannot say*
*I walk for miles*
*pretend to smile*
*I'm in denial every day*
*I'll cross the seas*
*I'm on my knees*
*You hear my pleas*
*but you can't stay*

*And I know you're leaving soon*
*And I'll be back here howling at the moon*
*waiting for the flowers*
*on mount saint helens to bloom*

*Walk with me*
*to the great blue sea*
*where the birds are free*
*and drift in the wind*
*That blows*
*when we walk the roads*
*where no one goes*
*and hope we don't begin*
*To scream and fight*
*That lasts all night*

*And have to make it right again*
*then with the sun*
*We'll know it's done*
*And there was no way we could win*

*And I'll send you down the road*
*I'll kiss your cheek and I'll let you go*
*when you're gone, I will explode*
*you'll see the plume*
*and feel the boom*

*Sometime down the rails*
*and the dusty trails*
*I'll tell the tales*
*of how we met*
*a freezing day*
*beneath the grey*
*I was astray*
*and I was wet*
*We've come too far*
*we're in our hearts*
*And if we part*
*we won't forget*
*so chase your dreams*
*I know it seems*
*it will redeem*
*all your regrets*

*And I know you're leaving soon*
*And I'll be back here howling at the moon*
*waiting for the flowers*
*on mount saint helens to bloom*

## Praying for Fire
## 2010

There's nothing going on in town this afternoon
so we polish up the truck and wait for the moon.
and the night passes by and everything's fine
so we polish up the truck, give it a shine
and we check all the fluids and change out a tire
we polish up the truck and we pray for fire.

The ping pong table is starting to wear
and we stop keeping score because we don't really care
we raise up the boom and shoot hoops from the ladder
but we don't keep score because it just don't matter
there's no referee and there's no umpire
and you don't keep score when you're praying for fire.

It hasn't rained a drop in 81 days
the whole damn valley is waiting to blaze
a spark could burn this place down to the ground
this whole damn valley is dead and brown
in my 21 years it's never been dryer
we're bored to tears and we're praying for fire

The wind kicks up; it's electrical storming
the bell finally rings when it hits a transformer
the storm brings thunder but it doesn't bring rains
and the bell finally rings when someone sees flames
it doesn't take long to see the problem is dire
the bell finally rings and we got us a fire.

*Like a house made a matches the whole town caught*
*we got the truck rolling but it couldn't be fought*
*people were running to the outskirts of town*
*we got the truck pumping but it couldn't be drown*
*our city was burning 'twas a sight to admire*
*we had the truck running but we couldn't beat fire.*

*The stores on main street now are blackened and haunted*
*we prayed for fire but this ain't what we wanted*
*gone are the places where we first fell in love*
*we prayed for a fire, not for wrath from above*
*it just kept spreading like a terminal cancer*
*we prayed for fire and our prayers were answered*

### Rain Ain't Fallin'
### 2010

The rain ain't fallin
the river ain't rising
trucks aren't haulin
and the plant ain't hiring
it's closing its doors
and it's leaving this town
and the rain ain't fallin' down
and the rain ain't fallin' down
There ain't no work here to be
found
And the rain ain't fallin' down

The rain ain't fallin
The flowers won't bloom
The ghost are calling
From the family tomb
Their bodies are dust
And the fields are brown
And the rain ain't fallin' down
The rain ain't fallin down
ain't no way a man could drown
And the rain ain't fallin' down

The rain ain't fallin
it won't even try
ain't a goddamn cloud
In the goddamn sky
we were thirsty then parched

then famished and dry
wondering why oh why
The worlds on Fire
The world's on fire
The world's on fire

They say the rain's fallin
someplace down the line
The creeks are swollen
And the water is wine

## Somebody New
## 2012

I've been thrown under buses
I've fallen through the cracks
I've been abandoned in the rushes
I've been stabbed in the back
there's not much out there honey
my heart has not been through
I've got to be somebody, be
somebody
be somebody new I don't know
who

I've seen a lot of basements
I've wandered through the halls
of empty baseball stadiums
and the nation's Capital
I've done some things honey
I never can undo
I want to be somebody, be
somebody
be somebody new, I don't know
who

I've told a lot of stories
I've spun some crazy tales
caught a couple minnows once
and turned them into whales
I've told so many lies
I've lost track of what is true

I want to be somebody be
somebody
be somebody new

maybe I could be a soldier
fight the enemy within
everyday I'm getting bolder
I may not win

I'm sorry if you trusted me
and I fucked everything up
tonight I think the holy grail
is just a coffee cup
and I know that I can't make it
up to you
I'd like to be somebody be
somebody
be somebody new I don't know
who

## River Road
## *2013*

*Walk me down the river road*
*Help me shoulder up my load*
*Soothe my anger and my hate*
*Mamma I'm not thinkin' straight*
*Keep me free from harm*
*Where the water is warm*
*I know everything will be alright*
*When that river is in sight*

*Pick me up and help me pass*
*I'm barefoot on broken glass*
*Shield me from the flying stones*
*Help me mend my broken bones*
*Lay my body on the stoop*
*Of the captain of the sloop*
*I know everything will be alright*
*When that river is in sight*

*Tell me that you're still my friend*
*Help me laugh and smile again*
*Tell me you'll stay by my side*
*Help me find a place to hide*
*Break me from these stocks*
*And take me to the docks*
*I know everything will be alright*
*When that river is in sight*

**Short Poem**
**2015**

There's so much in the world I'd prefer to avoid
Paranoid people make me paranoid
People in power are rigging the game
But if I had any power, I'd probably do the same

Point your guns at my sticks and I'll stick to my guns
I haven't gone crazy, but I did visit once
I'm not a guy who does what he's told
I've often been bought but I've never been sold

 I met a runaway priest in a hospital gown
He said "I'm starting to think Jesus doesn't want to be found"
I can't say I blame him after what he's been through
If I'd been crucified I'd be a little shy too

My fortune teller was a little bit vague
As to why exactly I end up at the Hague
The nighttime is a blanked that stretches the poles
When I look up at the sky I wonder who poked the holes

**Country Swing**
**2015**

I wish we could sing on the old country swing
And stomp our bare feet on the boards
I wish we could dance through the night on the ranch
By light of the moon on the porch
All of those times are just mem'ries
All of those songs are just ghosts
Our laughter is the sound that still haunts the grounds
Of the places that we love the most

If I could run through that old country sun
With sweat and dust on my brow
My shoulders are tan and my calloused hands
are tired from pushing the plow
They say that this country is dying
but only time can tell
the thing I miss most about my country home
is the way that the morning would smell

If I could walk on that old country dock
I'd hang my feet in the pond
If I could talk in that old country drawl
I'd whisper to you until dawn
Everyone here has their secrets
Everyone's burying facts
They're written on the page that we turn as we age
And never can turn back

## *The End of the World*
## *2017*

*I'm waiting for you to see me and smile*
*You know that I tell all the worst jokes*
*I view the world through the lens of denial*
*And I make friends with all the worst folks*

*I breathe the same air as all these adults*
*Somehow it gave me such different results*
*We walked in the rain 'til your hair it was curled*
*I'll laugh with you 'til the end of the world*

*Babe, you're like a sun that rises*
*An indian summer that won't yield to fall*
*You're always so full of surprises*
*Sometimes it's like I don't know you at all*

*My love for you grows wild like fern*
*Your pheromones gave me chemical burn*
*We ran down the dock by the sea and we twirled*
*I'll laugh with you 'til the end of the world*

*For now, my love, it looks like I'm staying*
*The shape of my car is in the grass of your yard*
*Who gives a damn what the neighbors are saying*
*I'm tired of living my life on my guard*

*I hope tomorrow will bring something new*
*If it does not, then that's ok too*
*History's a blanket that's knitted and purled*
*And I'll laugh with you 'til the end of the world*

*The End of the World Part 2*
*2017*

*I hope that you hope that I'm leavin' soon*
*because  I'm leaving soon either way*
*I'll run through the night by the light of the moon*
*And I'll be gone by the day*
*This world, you know it's beautiful*
*but lately it just makes me sad*
*baby, you stay for as long as you'd like*
*I'm leaving before it gets bad*

*Honey, I want you to want me to leave*
*I hate these drawn out goodbyes*
*around every turn there's new news to grieve*
*I'm fighting the tears from my eyes*
*Good is battling evil again*
*I'm not sure if good's gonna win*
*Hell yea I'm panicked, we're on the titanic*
*And water is pouring in*

*Girl, I'm begging you to beg me to go*
*it's hard to walk out the door*
*the tears of fear are starting to flow*
*I can't hold them back anymore*
*Fate holds our feet to the fires again*
*And soon it could mean our demise*
*As I understand it there's billions of planets*
*So who cares if one of 'em dies*

Special thanks to Doug Denison for reading
these stories and providing editorial guidance,
Monica Griffin for designing the cover art, and
Dan Vado for advising in the printing process.

www.ingramcontent.com/pod-product-compliance
Lightning Source LLC
Chambersburg PA
CBHW062009040426

42447CB00010B/1982